BOOKS BY REINHOLD NIEBUHR

The Irony of American History
Faith and History
Discerning the Signs of the Times
The Children of Light and the Children of Darkness
The Nature and Destiny of Man (ONE VOLUME EDITION)
Christianity and Power Politics
Beyond Tragedy
An Interpretation of Christian Ethics
Moral Man and Immoral Society

CHRISTIAN REALISM
AND
POLITICAL PROBLEMS

Christian Realism and Political Problems

BY REINHOLD NIEBUHR

New York

CHARLES SCRIBNER'S SONS

1953

To my friend, comrade, and colleague,
JOHN C. BENNETT,
with gratitude

PREFACE

THIS IS A COLLECTION OF ESSAYS on political, social, ethical, and theological themes. Many of the essays are published for the first time in these pages. One of them, dealing with the political thought of Augustine, is an elaboration of a lecture given at Columbia University on the Frances Carroll Memorial Lecture Foundation. The Chapter on "The Christian Witness in the Social and National Order" was originally given as an address before the World Council of Churches' First General Assembly, held in Amsterdam in 1948, and appeared in *The Chaplain*, December 10, 1948. The other essays which have been previously published in various journals, are reproduced by the kind permission of the editors of those journals as follows: "Democracy, Secularism, and Christianity" appeared in *Christianity and Crisis*, March 2, 1953; "Why Is Communism Evil?", while written for the book, appeared in *The New Leader*, June 8, 1953; "Coherence, Incoherence, and Christian Faith" appeared in *The Journal of Religion*, Vol. XXXI, No. 3, July 1951; "Love and Law in Protestantism and Catholicism" appeared in *The Journal of Religious Thought*, Vol. 9, No. 2, Spring-Summer 1952; "The Illusion of World Government" appeared in *Foreign Affairs*, April 1949; "The Anomaly of European Socialism" appeared in *The Yale Review*, Vol. XLII, No. 2, December 1952. The quotations from St. Augustine are taken from the Random House edition of *Basic Writings of St. Augustine*, edited by Whitney J. Oates.

REINHOLD NIEBUHR

CONTENTS

CHRISTIAN REALISM
AND
POLITICAL PROBLEMS

1. Faith and the Empirical Method in Modern Realism

AN OPENING WORD for this volume of essays on theological, ethical, and political themes may be helpful, if only in persuading the reader that, though the essays are on a variety of themes, they have a unity because they seek to establish the relevance of the Christian faith to contemporary problems, particularly to ethical and political ones. The central issue around which the various essays revolve or which they seek to illumine in its various facets, is fairly well explicated in the essay on the political realism of Augustine. This essay makes it clear that it is not assumed in these pages that the Christian faith will endow the believer with a superior wisdom which will enable him to escape errors, miscalculations, and faulty analyses of the common life of man. On the contrary, it is affirmed that most of the Christian theories before and after Augustine committed grievous errors in their analyses of the human situation and in resulting political calculations; and that Augustine himself must be subjected to criticism on various counts. He is presented as a significant figure, however, because he manages to escape some of the obvious errors in both Christian and secular theories, and does so, not fortuitously but upon the basis of an interpretation of human selfhood (and a concomitant theory of the egotism of which the self is guilty) which enables him to view the heights of human creativity and the depths of human destructiveness, which avoids the errors of moral sentimentality and cynicism, and their alternate corruptions of political systems of both secular and Christian thinkers.

It is one of the characteristics of a so-called scientific culture that it will rule out any theory whether of human nature or the human community which is based upon explicit or even implicit Christian presuppositions. Why should a culture which is so diligent in a scientific examination of everything from the geological ages to the human psyche, bother with any theory which confesses to, or even is suspected of, religious presuppositions? For is not this theory damned by its reliance upon a world-view which is, in the esteem of the modern man, *ueberwunderner standpunkt?*

Unfortunately for the validity of such a dismissal, the modern "scientific" examinations of the human scene are, upon close analysis, embarrassed by two considerations:

first they betray the influence of certain religious or ultimate presuppositions which are no less potent for being
unconfessed and no more true for being regarded as scientific. It is, in fact, impossible to examine the details of the
human picture without assuming a framework of meaning
for the details. The idea of a presuppositionless science
of human affairs is one of the points where the humanities
have been unduly influenced by the physical sciences, or
have falsely attempted to transfer the methods of the
latter to the former realm. The religious presuppositions
which form the framework for most modern scientific examinations of the human scene contain two very dubious
articles, which must be held responsible for most of the
errors and illusions in these examinations: A) The idea of
the perfectability of man and B) the idea of progress. The
errors into which the examination is betrayed are reinforced
by a characteristic method of the inquiry. That method
is to examine man as if he were no more than one of the
many objects in nature, which the scientific method will
be able to comprehend fully, if only its tools are sufficiently precise and the scientist is sufficiently objective.

Any careful observation of any structure of reality,
of sequences and causes, even if its frame of reference is
inadequate, will yield some truth. It is therefore not surprising that modern social and psychological sciences have
been able to teach us a great deal about man and his community. But it is also significant that these disciplines have
been fruitful of many errors and illusions on the ultimate
level. These errors are the second reason for questioning

the certainties of modern culture. Its conclusions do not conform to the obvious facts of human experience. They are held to the more desperately as this contradiction is noted by a stray non-conformist and dissenter. The fact that the presuppositions have determined the conclusions is obscured by the insistence that the conclusions have been arrived at by empirical, or "scientific" observation. The prestige of the "scientific method" plays a part in giving authority to the modern creed, analogous to the service which the priestly incantations had in establishing the creeds of more explicitly religious eras. Significantly "scientific" has two connotations. It means "empirical" or an attitude of "humility before the fact," or the inductive rather than the deductive method. It also, somewhat strangely, means "rational" which could imply that empirical methods must avail themselves of strictly logical tools to avoid caprice; but it may also imply that rational coherence is regarded as the test of truth. In the latter case the two connotations of scientific, "empirical" and "rational," would stand in contradiction; because the test of rational coherence might prompt men to deny obvious facts because they violated, or appeared to violate, the test of rational coherence. It is particularly important to note this in the study of man, who is both a creature and creator and who does not fit easily into any system of rational or natural coherence. The second reason why it would behoove modern culture to be more receptive to analyses of human behavior which reveal Christian, rather than modern presuppositions, is that the modern culture, despite all of its boasted empiricism has been caught in some obvious miscalculations and even in some tragic errors. The world is not at all as the eighteenth century hoped it would be if men would only disavow their ir-relevant other-worldly hopes and expend all their energies on the perfecting of man and his society. The simplest way of defining this contradiction between past hopes and present realities is to call attention to the fact that the heaven on earth of modern man turned out to be more incredible than the old heaven; and much more danger-ous. Furthermore, it is an obvious datum about the char-acter of man that even the most explicitly "irreligious" should have been so intent upon building such incredible utopias.

It may seem unfair to cite the horrible evils of the communist utopia as a refutation of the many dreams of a liberal culture, for there are marked differences between the soft utopianism of the liberal world and the hard uto-pianism of communism. But it is not unfair to call atten-tion to the similarities underneath the differences and to note that in almost every instance the communist evil is rooted in miscalculations which are shared by modern liberal culture but which have not fortunately produced such evil fruit because there has been no political program for implementing the illusions, and because the diffusion of power in the democratic world as distinguished from the monopoly of power, provided in Marxism, tends to check illusions by contrasting truths or errors. So the lib-eral world manages to achieve a tolerable life in a kind

of confusion of purposes, which is better than the organization of the whole resources of a community for the
achievement of false ends.

Since this volume is devoted to the question of realism and is critical of the lack of realism in contemporary
culture as compared to Christian "realism," we may well
begin with the differences in presuppositions which may
account for this difference. According to the Christian
view, the human self arises as an independent and self-
determining force in the very social process and historical
continuum, in which it is also a creature. Its freedom is
a radical one because the self is not easily brought under
the control of reason just as it is not easily kept within
the confines of nature's harmonies. This freedom is the
basis of the self's destructive as well as creative powers;
and there is no simple possibility of making nice distinctions between human destructiveness and creativity. In
the words of Pascal, the "dignity of man and his misery"
have the same source. Man stands perpetually outside and
beyond every social, natural, communal, and rational cohesion. He is not bound by any of them which makes for
his creativity; he is tempted to make use of all of them
for his own ends. That is the basis of his destructiveness.
One may go further and declare that the limitless character of man's ideals of perfection and the inordinancy of
human lusts and ambitions have their common root in
the capacity of man to stand out of, and survey any, historical or natural situation which surrounds him. The
notorious failure to anticipate or to explain any form of

inordinancy, more particularly the lusts and ambitions revealed in modern demonic religio-political movements, is
certainly related to the preconceptions which prompt the
various forms of modern culture to coordinate man to
some system of nature or of reason. Consider the various
miscalculations of nature and the degree of this inordinancy in various disciplines. The psychiatrists, at least the
Freudians among them, are inclined to attribute every
form of inordinancy to "hypertrophy" of impulses, caused
by the check upon natural expression of impulsive drives
by the restraints of civilization. The clash of human interests is defined as caused by "aggressiveness"; and various schemes are projected for its elimination. They all
seem singularly irrelevant in a day in which we face a
form of religio-political mania which is obviously compounded by utopian dreams and power lusts, completely
out of the dimension of the impulses which are thus
brought under prospective control.

At any rate, the belief that the power of man's lusts
and ambitions is no more than some sub-rational impulse,
which can be managed with more astute social engineering or more psychiatric help, lends an air of sentimentality
and unreality to the political opinions of the liberal world.

Even more important is the difference between Christian and modern presuppositions in regard to the issue
of the universality of man's tendency to egocentricity. The
Christian insistence on its universality would seem to be
attested by practical experience about as irrefutably as
any truth can be established. It is empirically respected

by all men of affairs who are charged with any responsibility in business or government. But academic "empiricism" insists that the Christian conviction rests upon
a dogmatic assumption, rather than upon evidence. It
therefore proceeds to uncover evidence that particular
forms of egocentricity are the consequence of particular
causes. This is indeed a fact. But preoccupation with this
fact tempts a scientific culture to obscure the more general
human phenomenon which underlies the particular social
and psychic causes of particularly excessive or unique
forms of egotism. Thus an elaborate scientific enterprise
may result in a totally unjustified nominalism, unable to
apprehend general and universal characteristics under obviously unique phenomenon.

It is no doubt interesting to distinguish the historic
roots and the peculiar forms which ambition and the lust
for power may take, let us say, in the lives of a Chinese
Buddhist abbot, a Prussian general, an American go-get-
ter, and a Russian commissar. It is also important to distinguish the degrees of social evil in each one of the phenomena. But it would be rather "unscientific" to ignore
the common element in all of these forms of ambition; or
to obscure the fact that the power lusts of men of power,
the vanity of beautiful women, and the envy of scholars
betray common characteristics, in spite of great differences. The now generally despised Marxist theory which
attributes egotism to the institution of property and hopes
to redeem mankind by abolishing this economic institution, is but a crude form of the "scientific" effort to find

particular causes of particular evils, which characterize our modern culture, and which almost invariably results in ascribing a general human tendency to a particular cause.

It is rather typical of the errors to which modern thought is beguiled by the tendencies of a scientific nominalism that modern psychiatry in its various schools can know so much about the complexities of the human psyche and should have such great success therapeutically, and yet should be involved in the error of assuming that the universal tendency to egocentricity must be due to faulty education; and that it could be overcome either by adequate psychiatric technic or by teaching mothers to give their children "uncritical love." The fact that the phenomenon of self-seeking may be related, not to specific forms of insecurity but to the insecurity of life itself, seems to be obscured in even the most sophisticated psychological theory, which is why psychological theories are so irrelevant to political theory; for politics must, in the words of Hume, take the egotism of men for granted.

It is equally typical of our nominalistic culture, so intent upon finding specific causes for general tendencies, that the most noted philosopher of America should attribute the egoistic corruption in moral and political judgments, which men of affairs take for granted and discount in their daily life, to the supposed compromise in the battle between science and authority, in which the fields of politics and morals were presumably declared immune to the beneficent sway of science, and kept under the traditional authorities of Church and state. In this case an elaborate theory is invented by a respected philosopher to account for a common phenomenon which the common sense of mankind has long since recognized as a universal characteristic, requiring no detailed explanations.

The involvement of man in the same historical process in which he is also an agent, must account for the egoistic corruptions of his judgments in all human affairs and conflicts. The double relation of man to the historical process in which he is both creature and creator, is in fact responsible for many errors in the political theories of modern culture. This is a problem for which there is no easy solution upon the basis of any presuppositions. The Christian presuppositions do, however, tend to guard the sense of the unity of man in both dimensions and to warn against the pretension of obscuring his status as a creature and imagining himself purely the creator of historical destiny. By contrast, the errors, due to the miscalculations of man's status in history, are various. The *laissez-faire* theories, to which the business classes of the Western world are so devoted, are based upon physiocratic theories, according to which there is no essential difference between nature and history; and men are warned not to interfere with the "laws of nature" which govern both. Naturally this theory fails to anticipate the various forms of inordinancy in human ambitions which distinguish man from nature; or to measure the endlessly unique forms of historic occasions for which man must contrive unique answers. The contrasting presupposition, one form of which communism

inherited from Marx, and the liberal world derived from
the thought of Comte, shares with the first the conviction
that man is a part of nature and tends to obscure that
dignity of the human spirit which distinguishes him from
nature and makes it impossible and wrong to "manipulate" him as nature is manipulated. But it also believes
that some men have the ability (according to Comte and
the scientific humanism which derives from him) or the
destiny (according to Marxist theories) to master human
and historical destiny. These theories violate the "dignity"
of some men; and they fail to observe the creaturely limitations of the elite who are assigned to the role of masters
of history. In the case of communism, the fortunate or unfortunate realization of the dreams of mastering history
discloses the dangers in the pretensions of wisdom and
disinterestedness, which are made by an elite. It proves
that no one is good or wise enough to be completely entrusted with the destiny of his fellowmen. Unfortunately,
this clear refutation of the policies, which rest upon the
presupposition that human history can and must be mastered, had not deterred bold scientists in the liberal world
from projecting various scientific programs for manipu-
lating historical events as if they were in the dimension
of nature. (Chapter 2 on world government in this volume
analyzes one such project.)

All these theories are based upon erroneous estimates
of the disinterestedness and the wisdom of the mind which
is called upon to manage the stuff of community and history, and of the maleability of the stuff which is to be

managed. They must therefore be regarded as variants of the classical dualism of Plato and Aristotle, no matter how explicit their anti-Aristotelian or anti-Platonic tendencies. The fact of this similarity, despite superficial obvious differences, leads one to assume that modern theories are as intent upon bringing complex facts of human nature and history into some system of rational coherence as classical thought; and that they lack empirical accuracy on account of this passion for rational coherence. (This is why I thought an essay on "Coherence, Incoherence, and the Christian Faith" would be relevant to this series of essays, though most of the essays are devoted to political themes.)

Perhaps it is indicative of the similarities underneath the differences between classical rationalism and modern pragmatism (with its ostensible rejection of a transcendent mind for a merely technical rational function) that John Dewey in his "Common Faith" expects the scientific method to achieve a universally valid viewpoint, closely akin to the services which Aristotle's *nous* accomplished. He attributed particular viewpoints to traditional prejudices and historic religions, and hoped that the "methods of science" would resolve them, so that "men of good will" would reach practical unanimity on the goals of life. It must be regarded as an ironic refutation of this hope that shortly after it was eloquently stated, the world community became divided between warring political creeds, each of which believed their convictions to be validated by science; and that there should be, in modern political conflicts, less respect for a common humanity, and less concern for justice to individuals without regard to their position as friends or foes, than in the traditional cultures which thought less of a universal humanity than our culture, but had a greater sense of pity for the persons who are caught in the warfare between the fragmentary purposes and communities of mankind.

It might be noted that, without a sense of the universality of an egocentric corruption, the passion for a universal humanity quickly degenerates into hatred for those who express their egotism in some ways, different from our own. The force of humility and pity no longer operates to bind men together despite their differing interests and convictions. Stoic idealism degenerated in somewhat the same fashion. It began with appreciation for all men because they possesed a common reason; and ended with condescension for those who did not have a full measure of rational endowment.

I must add that several essays in this volume deal with current political problems in our own nation; and I allow myself various judgments in them which I would not care to designate as "Christian" except in the sense that they are made by one who obviously holds Christian convictions. It is necessary to say this because much confusion is caused in both Catholic and Protestant circles by the effort to claim some ultimate sanction for what must always be hazardous and tentative opinions. In this tendency I can see little difference between some theologians and some modern scientists. Both of them tend to appeal to what is to them an ultimate authority to sanction judgments which do not flow inevitably from either the Christian faith or from the "scientific method."

Some of the essays betray a critical attitude toward Marxism in both its democratic variety and in its communist form. I have always resisted the dangerous illusions of communism. But the notes of criticism on even democratic socialism are new. They may prove a lack of consistency but they also suggest a movement in our political and spiritual history, which influenced us all and which ought to persuade us the more to disavow pretensions of wisdom for any judgment of the moment. I would insist that the discrediting of the Marxist dogma in all of its varieties and not merely in its most noxious form, should convince us, not of the truth of contradictory dogmas, which it was the one virtue of Marxism to correct or to balance, but to be grateful for a democratic society which manages to extract a measure of truth from the contest of contrasting errors. We have all felt that a democratic society was most compatible with the Christian faith, but a pietistic inheritance in our evangelical tradition persuaded us that its chief virtue was its safeguarding of the individual. We should realize in this age of the rise of noxious political religions that it has another great resource from the standpoint of the Christian outlook. It provides for checks and balances upon the pretensions of men as well as upon their lust for power; it thereby prevents truth from turning into falsehood when the modicum of error in truth is not challenged and the modicum of truth in a falsehood is not rescued and cherished.

2. *The Illusion of World Government*

THE TRUSTFUL ACCEPTANCE of false solutions for our per-
plexing problems adds a touch of pathos to the tragedy
of our age.

The tragic character of our age is revealed in the
world-wide insecurity which is the fate of modern man.
Technical achievements, which a previous generation had
believed capable of solving every ill to which the human
flesh is heir, have created, or at least accentuated, our
insecurity. For the growth of technics has given the perennial problems of our common life a more complex form
and a scope that has grown to be world-wide.

Our problem is that technics have established a rudimentary world community but have not integrated it organically, morally or politically. They have created a com-

munity of mutual dependence, but not one of mutual trust and respect. Without this higher integration, advancing technics tend to sharpen economic rivalries within a general framework of economic interdependence; they change the ocean barriers of yesterday into the battlegrounds of today; and they increase the deadly efficacy of the instruments of war so that vicious circles of mutual fear may end in atomic conflicts and mutual destruction. To these perplexities an ideological conflict has been added, which divides the world into hostile camps.

It is both necessary and laudable that men of good will should, in this situation, seek to strengthen every moral and political force which might give a rudimentary world community a higher degree of integration. It was probably inevitable that the desperate plight of our age should persuade some well meaning men that the gap between a technically integrated and politically divided community could be closed by the simple expedient of establishing a world government through the fiat of the human will and creating world community by the fiat of world government. It is this hope which adds a touch of pathos to already tragic experiences. The hope not only beguiles some men from urgent moral and political responsibilities. It tempts others into irresponsible criticisms of the necessarily minimal constitutional structure which we have embodied in the United Nations and which is as bad as its critics aver only if a better one is within the realm of possibilities.

Virtually all arguments for world government rest

upon the simple presupposition that the desirabilty of
world order proves the attainability of world government.
Our precarious situation is unfortunately no proof, either
of the moral ability of mankind to create a world government by an act of the will, nor of the political ability of
such a government to integrate a world community in
advance of a more gradual growth of the "social tissue"
which every community requires more than government.

Most advocates of world government also assume
that nations need merely follow the alleged example of
the individuals of another age who are supposed to have
achieved community by codifying their agreements into
law and by providing an agency of some kind for law
enforcement. This assumption ignores the historic fact
that the mutual respect for each other's rights in particular communities is older than any code of law; and
that machinery for the enforcement of law can be efficacious only when a community as a whole obeys its laws
implicitly, so that coercive enforcement may be limited
to a recalcitrant minority.

The fallacy of world government can be stated in
two simple propositions. The first is that governments are
not created by fiat (though sometimes they can be im-
posed by tyranny). The second is that governments have
only limited efficacy in integrating a community.

II

The advocates of world government propose calling

a world constitutional convention which would set up the machinery of a global constitutional order and would then call upon the nations to abrogate or abridge their sovereignty in order that this newly created universal sovereignty could have unchallenged sway. No such explicit abnegation has ever taken place in the history of the world. Explicit governmental authority has developed historically from the implicit authority of patriarchal or matriarchal tribal forms. Governments, so established, have extended their dominion over weaker neighbors. But the abridgment of sovereignty has always been indirect rather than direct; or it has been attained by the superimposition of power.

The notion that world government is a fairly simple possibility is the final and most absurd form of the "social contract" conception of government which has confused modern political thought since Hobbes. It must certainly be obvious by this time that the conception of a state of nature in which all men were at war with all, and of a subsequent social contract through which men established a power over themselves to avoid mutual annihilation, is a pure fiction. A small human community is as primordial as the individual. No group of individuals have ever created either government or community out of whole cloth. One reason why the social contract conception of government has a particular plausibility with us is because the United States came closer to a birth by "contract" than any other nation. But the preamble of our constitution declares that its purpose is to establish a "more perfect

union." That is a very telling phrase which presupposes
a previous union. This previous union was in fact established on the battlefield in a common struggle against a
common foe; it needed only to be made "more perfect."
It may be observed in passing that, though the thirteen
colonies had never enjoyed sovereignty, they did not find
it too easy to submit what had only been potential, and
not actual, sovereignty to the authority of the federal
union. We fought a civil war before it was proved that
they had in fact done this without reservations.

When the question is raised whether the nations of
the world would voluntarily first create, and then submit
to, a super-national authority, the possible reluctance of
nations, other than Russia, to take this step is fortunately
or unfortunately obscured by the Russian intransigeance.
The Russians have declared again and again that they
would leave the United Nations if the veto power were
abolished. This means that Russia, as a prospective minority in a world community, is not ready to submit her fate
to the will of a majority, even in such a loose organization
as the United Nations. It is therefore obvious that she
would be even more unwilling to submit her sovereignty
to a more highly integrated constitutional order.

The proponents of world government have two answers to the problem posed by Russian intransigeance.
One is to assert that the Russians never have had the
chance to accept or reject a genuinely constitutional world
order; and that there are real possibilities of her acceptance of a constitution which is not weighted against her.

This answer contains in a nutshell the rationalist illusion implicit in world government theories. It assumes that constitutions can insure the mutual trust upon which community rests. Actually, even the best constitution must, if it be democratic, set up some kind of majority rule. It is not workable if there is not enough common ground between majority and minority to assure that a majority will not take advantage of a minority, or that the minority will not suspect the majority of injustice, even though without cause. There are republics in South America with quite nice constitutions in which a defeated minority starts conspiracies against the government, usually through military channels, on the day after election.

The other answer to the problem of Russian intransigeance is a proposed creation of a "world" government without Russia. Thus in the name of "one world" the world would be divided in two. Proponents of world government are always ready with criticisms of the ambiguities in the Charter of the United Nations, without recognizing that those ambiguities correspond to the actual historical situation. The Security Council is, for instance, a bridge of a sort between the segments of a divided world. They would destroy that bridge for the sake of creating a more logical constitutional system. This done, they look forward to one of two possibilities.

One is that Russia, faced with a united opposition, and concluding that she would not have to sacrifice her communist Government but only her ambition to spread communism, would ultimately capitulate and join the world federation. This abstract approach to political problems is completely oblivious of the dynamism of communism.

The other course chosen by some advocates of world government is to create such a government without Russia and to divide the world more consistently in the name of the principle of "one" world. If this should lead to a world conflict they believe that the agonies of war will be assuaged for us by our knowledge that we are at least fighting for a principle of ultimate validity.

There is, of course, a possibility that a closer political integration of the non-communist nations may save the world from war by the creation of an adequate preponderance of power in the west. But such an objective is not to be reached by loftily disavowing "power politics" in favor of "law." The world federalists who accept the inevitability of war walk bravely up the hill of pure idealism and down again into the realm of pure power politics. In this journey they rid themselves of the logical and moral ambiguities of the much despised quasi-constitutional system of the United Nations. Their brethren who are in a less exalted frame of mind will continue to put up with the Charter for the sake of preserving a bridge, however slight, between Russia and the west, making the best arrangements they can to restrain Russia, while trying at the same time to strengthen the existing world security agencies.

The ambiguities in the Charter of the United Nations which so outrage the advocates of world government are in fact the consequence of seeking to guarantee two, rather than one, objectives. The one objective is to preserve the unity of one world, even though it be seriously divided, and to provide a meeting ground between east and west where some of the tensions and frictions may be resolved. The other is to preserve the integrity of our "way of life" against a tyrannical system which we abhor. The Russians, in so far as they are honest devotees of a Marxist dream of world order, are presumably in the same position. Each of us hopes ultimately to create a world order upon the basis of our conception of justice. Neither of us is ready, at the moment, to submit our fate to a world authority without reservation, so long as the possibility remains that such an authority could annul a system of law and justice to which we are deeply committed.

III

So far we have considered only the difficulties of creating a world government by constitutional fiat. But a much more serious defect in world government theories is to be found in their conception of the relation of government to community. Governments cannot create communities for the simple reason that the authority of government is not primarily the authority of law nor the authority of force, but the authority of the community itself. Laws are obeyed because the community accepts them as corresponding, on the whole, to its conception of justice. This is particularly true of democratically organized communities. But it is well to observe that even in traditional, non-democratic communities of the past there was a discernible difference between tyranny and legitimate government. It consisted precisely in the fact that a legitimate government relied primarily upon the implicit consent of the community.

Even in a national constitutional system, such as our own, we have seen how limited is the power of law whenever a portion of the community adheres to moral standards which differ from those of the total community. We have had this experience both with the prohibition movement and with the question of civil rights for Negroes in southern states. And where is the police force, loyal to a world state, to come from? The police power of a government cannot be a pure political artifact. It is an arm of the community's body. If the body is in pieces, the arm cannot integrate it.

The priority of the community to its laws and its use of force does not mean that both law and force may not have limited efficacy in perfecting the organization and preserving the integrity of the community. Good constitutions provide for the rational arbitrament of many conflicting and competing forces which might otherwise tear the community apart. Preponderant force in one part of the community may also so shape the social forces of the total community that its use need not be perpetual. Thus the preponderant force of the northern states decided the issue whether our nation was a nation or merely a federation of states. But force is no longer necessary to guarantee the loyalty of the southern states to our union. The ancient empires of Egypt, Babylon and Persia were created through the preponderant force of a particular city-state; but they finally achieved a unity which did not require the constant application of force. It must be noted that this pattern of coalescence of communities gives us no analogy for the creation of a world community in democratic terms, that is, without the imposition of preponderant power. The best analogy for our present world situation is to be found in Greece rather than in Egypt or Babylon. The Greek city-states never achieved the imperial unity of the oriental empires. The threat of Persia did finally prompt the organization of the Delian League; but the rivalry of Sparta and Athens for the hegemony in the League resulted in its disintegration. The unity of Greece was finally achieved under Philip and Alexander of Macedon. But this imperial unity was also a tyrannical nemesis for Greek culture. The analogy in present global terms would be the final unification of the world through the preponderant power of either America or Russia, whichever proved herself victorious in a final global struggle. The analogy teaches us nothing about the possibilities of a constitutional world state. It may teach us that though the perils of international anarchy are very great, they may still be preferable to international tyranny.

The coalescence of communities from city-states to empires in the ancient world, and from feudal entities to nations in the modern period, was frequently accomplished only by the imposition of preponderant power.

The fact is particularly significant, since all of these communities could rely upon all sorts of "organic" factors for their force of cohesion which the rudimentary world community lacks. By organic factors, I mean such forces as the power of ethnic kinship, the force of a common history—particularly the memory of joint struggles against a common foe—a common language, a common culture and a common religion. We do have examples of ethnically and religiously pluralistic nations and empires, but they possess a basic homogeneity of some kind, underlying the differences. In modern India, where religious differences are thoroughgoing and highly localized, it proved impossible to construct a constitutional system which could allay the mutual fears of Hindus and Moslems. The birth in blood of these two nations, once the unifying force of an imperial power was removed, ought to teach our world planners more about the limited efficacy of constitutions than they have evidently learned. There were certainly more common elements in the situation in India than the world community will possess for a long time to come. Despite these common elements, the unity of India proved to be unattainable.

Sometimes the world planners recognize the absence of organic forces of cohesion in the world community. Thus Erich Kahler[1] sees that a world constitution lacks the "substratum" of organic and historical forces, which characterize the constitutions of national governments.

[1]Erich Kahler, "The Question of a 'Minimum Constitution.'" *Common Cause*, June, 1948.

But he draws the conclusion that a world constitution "must create the substratum to which it is to be applied." The proposed method of creating the substratum, according to Mr. Kahler, is to use "regions" rather than "extant states" as electoral units in the world constitution, for "if we base the world government on the states, we will fail in the essential task of creating the substratum." The illusions of omnipotence which infect the thought of this kind of political idealism could not be more vividly portrayed. There is no explanation of how states, who have a sovereign voice, would be persuaded to grant this electoral power to "regions" which would have no such voice in a world constitutional convention. The idea probably is that there would be a nonrepresentative constitutional convention of "experts" and the hope is that sovereign states will meekly accept the dictum of the experts that regions offer a better "substratum" for the world community than extant states. Nor is any attempt made to deal with the difficulty that many of the regions which would hopefully be created are so little integrated that an electoral canvass would be completely meaningless in them.

The fact is that even the wisest statecraft cannot create social tissue. It can cut, sew and redesign social fabric to a limited degree. But the social fabric upon which it works must be "given."

IV

The international community is not totally lacking in

social tissue; but it is very scant, compared with that of particular states. Let us briefly assess the various factors in it. Most important as a force of social cohesion in the world community is the increasing economic interdependence of peoples of the world. But it is important to contrast this economic interdependence immediately with the wide disparity in the economic strength of various nations. At the climactic dinner of the World Republic convention, held in Chicago in October, 1948, Professor Urey, the atomic scientist, expressed the conviction that the "inclusion of the illiterate, poverty-stricken, overnumerous masses of the Far East" constituted the major problem of the world state. He believed that the white race would not tolerate being outvoted by Asiatics. He therefore proposed a system of weighted votes in favor of nations with high literacy and abundance of raw materials and industrial production. He felt certain that the more "enlightened" Orientals would not object to this procedure. But an objection, from Thomas Tchou, sitting two places to the left of Professor Urey, was immediately forthcoming. Weighted representation, he declared, was immoral.[2] Thus the real problems have an inconvenient habit of peeking through, even at a dinner of a World Republic convention.

A second factor in the social tissue of the world community is the fear of mutual annihilation, heightened in recent years by the new dimension which atomic discoveries have given to mankind's instruments of death. We

[2]*Common Cause*, December, 1948, p. 199.

must not underestimate this fear as a social force, even as we must recognize that some culturally pluralistic communities of past history have achieved some cohesion through the minimal conviction that order is to be preferred to anarchy. But the fear of destruction in itself is less potent than the fear of specific peril from a particular foe. There is no record in history of peoples establishing a common community because they feared each other, though there are many instances when the fear of a common foe acted as the cement of cohesion.

The final and most important factor in the social tissue of the world community is a moral one. Enlightened men in all nations have some sense of obligation to their fellow-men, beyond the limits of their nation-state. There is at least an inchoate sense of obligation to the inchoate community of mankind. The desperate necessity for a more integrated world community has undoubtedly increased this sense of obligation, inculcated in the conscience of mankind since the rise of universal, rather than parochial, philosophies and religions. This common moral sense is of tremendous importance for the moral and religious life of mankind; but it does not have as much immediate political relevance as is sometimes supposed. Political cohesion requires common convictions on particular issues of justice; and these are lacking. If there is a "natural law" which is "self-evident" to all men, it certainly does not contain very much specific content beyond such minimal rules as the prohibition of murder and theft and such general principles of justice as the dictum that each man is to have his due. There is little agreement on the criteria by which the due of each man is to be measured.

There is a special irony in the fact that the primary differences in the conceptions of justice in the world do not, however, spring from religious and cultural differences between east and west. They can therefore not be resolved by elaborate efforts at cultural syncretism between east and west. The primary differences arise from a civil war in the heart of western civilization, in which a fanatical equalitarian creed has been pitted against a libertarian one. This civil war has become nationally localized. Russia has become the national center of the equalitarian creed, while America is the outstanding proponent of the libertarian one. The common use of the word "democracy," together with the contradictory interpretations of the meaning of that word, is the semantic symbol of the conflict. The idea that this conflict could be resolved by greater semantic accuracy is, however, one of the illusions of a too rationalistic culture which fails to understand the power of the social forces expressed in contradictory symbols.

In short, the forces which are operating to integrate the world community are limited. To call attention to this fact does not mean that all striving for a higher and wider integration of the world community is vain. That task must and will engage the conscience of mankind for ages to come. But the edifice of government which we build will be sound and useful if its height is proportionate to the strength of the materials from which it is constructed.

The immediate political situation requires that we seek not only peace, but also the preservation of a civilization which we hold to be preferable to the universal tyranny with which Soviet aggression threatens us. Success in this double task is the goal; let us not be diverted from it by the pretense that there is a simple alternative.

We would, I think, have a better chance of success in our struggle against a fanatical foe if we were less sure of our purity and virtue. The pride and self-righteousness of powerful nations are a greater hazard to their success in statecraft than the machinations of their foes. If we could combine a greater degree of humility with our stubborn resolution, we might not only be more successful in holding the dyke against tyranny, but we might also gradually establish a genuine sense of community with our foe, however small. No matter how stubbornly we resist Russian pressure, we should still have a marginal sense of community with the Soviet Union, derived from our sense of being involved in a common fate of tragic proportions and from a recognition of a common guilt of mutual fear. If community in basic terms is established by various organic forces of history, it must finally be preserved by mutual forbearance and forgiveness.

There is obviously no political program which can offer us, in our situation, perfect security against either war or tyranny. Nevertheless, we are not prisoners of historical destiny. We shall have constant opportunity to perfect instruments of peace and justice if we succeed in creating some communal foundation upon which constitutional structures can rest. We shall exploit our opportunities the more successfully, however, if we have knowledge of the limits of the will in creating government, and of the limits of government in creating community. We may have pity upon, but can have no sympathy with, those who flee to the illusory security of the impossible from the insecurities and ambiguities of the possible.

3. *Why is Communism So Evil?*

WHAT MAKES COMMUNISM so evil and what are the sources
of its malignancy? We are bound to ask the question because we are fated as a generation to live in the insecurity
which this universal evil of communism creates for our
world. The timid spirits ask another question: is communism really as evil as we now think; or are we tempted
by the tensions of our conflict with it to exaggerate our
negative judgments about it, somewhat as we did in judg-
ing the Kaiser's Germany, which we erroneously regarded
as about as evil as Hitler's Germany subsequently proved
to be. It is important to analyze the nature of the communist evil both for the sake of those who take its evil
for granted but do not bother to diagnose its nature or

trace its sources; and for the sake of those deluded spirits who imagine that communism is but a different version of a common democratic creed, a difference which might be resolved if a dissipation of the war psychosis would permit us to engage in the enterprise. We must analyze it too for the sake of those who assess the degree of evil in communism correctly but prove their confusion in regard to its nature by comparing it with something much less evil than itself, as for instance the former State Department official who asserted that communism was "nothing but" the old Russian imperialism in a new form. This judgment obscured the difference between the comparatively ordinate and normal lust for power of a great traditional nation and the noxious demonry of this world wide secular religion.

If we seek to isolate the various causes of an organized evil which spreads terror and cruelty throughout the world and confronts us everywhere with faceless men who are immune to every form of moral and political suasion, we must inevitably begin with the monopoly of power which communism establishes. Disproportions of power anywhere in the human community are fruitful of injustice, but a system which gives some men absolute power over other men results in evils which are worse than injustice. Evidence drawn from the records of armies of occupation throughout history prove the deleterious effects of absolute power, impinging upon powerlessness, on both those who have power and those who lack it. We must draw a distinction between the theory which makes for a monopoly of power and the practical effects of such a monopoly. Socialists may, for instance, share a similar theory with communism; but while they are inserted into the wholesome balances of power of a democracy their actions and character are different than those of the communist oligarchs. On the other hand, socialists are wrong if they interpret present communist practices as merely the fortuitous corruption of the original Marxist ideals. Marxism did not indeed plan the highly centralized power structure of communism; but Marx did plan for a "dictatorship of the proletariat"; and the progressive moral deterioration of such a dictatorship was inevitable rather than fortuitous, for two reasons: The first is that when society is divided into the powerful and the powerless there is no way of preventing the gradual centralization of the monopoly of power. The monopoly of a class becomes the monopoly of the party which claims to be the vanguard of the whole class; the monopoly of the party gradually becomes the monopoly of a small oligarchy who speak at first for the class to other classes who have been robbed of power. But their authority inevitably degenerates into a monopoly of power exercised over their own party and class because no one in the whole community has the constitutional means to challenge and check the inevitable extension of power after which the most powerful grasp. The dictatorship of the oligarchy further degenerates into the dictatorship of a single tyrant. It was significant that a fallen oligarch, such as Trotsky, was as powerless as the most powerless peasant to challenge the

rule of the tyrant who had defeated him, or to amend
the history of the events written by the victor to justify
his victory and to discredit his foe. Another reason for
the excessive concentration of power is that the Marxist
theory wrongly assumes that economic power inheres
solely in the ownership of property and obscures the
power of the manager of property. It therefore wrongly
concludes that the socialization of property causes economic power to evaporate when in fact it merely gives
a single oligarchy a monopoly of both economic and political power. One pathetic consequence of this error is
that the workers of a socialized concern, who are in theory
the common owners of the property and are therefore prevented from holding any significant power, are rendered
powerless against the managerial oligarchs who run the
factory. The inevitable result is the accumulation of injustices more grievous than those which originally inspired
the Marxist revolt against a free society.

While the relation of absolute power to complete
defencelessness is the basic cause of all the evils of communism, it must be recognized that the communist tyranny
is supported and aggravated by the whole series of pretensions derived from the secular religion which creates
the ethos of the communist society. The most significant
moral pretension is derived from the utopian illusions of
Marxism. According to these illusions every policy of
Marxist propaganda and class conflict has the object of
hastening the day of historical climax when an ideal classless society will emerge. The utopian illusions presumably

make communism more dangerous rather than more evil. They are responsible for the loyalty of a group of intellectuals to the communist cause. The disillusionment of these idealists in Europe does not prevent a new crop of Asian intellectuals from being taken in by these pretensions. Furthermore, the illusions enable communists to pose as the liberators of every class or nation which they intend to enslave; and to exploit every moral and political weakness of the civilized world as if they had the conscience of civilization in their keeping. The utopian illusions undoubtedly make communism more dangerous than Nazism, which could not, for instance, have conquered either Poland or China by internal conspiracy. The power of the illusions is proved by the fact that the most consistent foes of communism feel themselves compelled to argue that it is as bad as Nazism, contending that the tyrannical practice is the same whatever the contradiction between the different theories of moral cynicism and utopianism which inspire them. These arguments imply that there is a virtue in the utopian ideal which the practice unfortunately belies. The fact is that the utopianism is the basis of the evil in communism as well as of its greater danger. It provides a moral facade for the most unscrupulous political policy, giving the communist oligarch the moral warrant to suppress and sacrifice immediate values in the historical process for the sake of reaching so ideal a goal. It may be unfair to compare the strain of utopianism in our liberal culture with the communist utopianism. But it is not unfair to suggest that the attractive power of communism for many so-called idealists is due to a general utopian element in our culture which fails to acknowledge the perennial moral contradictions on every level of historical advance.

We cannot suppose that the ruthless oligarchs in the Kremlin exercise their power without a measure of cynicism; but such are the powers of human self-deception that, for all we know, they may still be believers who persuade themselves that they are doing what they do for noble ultimate ends. Stalin is reported to have rebuffed a journalist who compared him with Napoleon. Napoleon, he declared, had no good purpose as the goal for which his power was the means. In one sense the presence or absence of cynicism among the oligarchs is beside the point. The important point is that the ruthless power operates behind a screen of pretended ideal ends, a situation which is both more dangerous and more evil than pure cynical defiance of moral ends. It corresponds to the weakness of the human heart more nearly than absolute cynicism, for men are less inclined to pure cynicism than to the delusion that they serve some noble purpose in engaging in projects which serve their own end.

The fierce self-righteousness derived from these utopian illusions is accentuated by the Marxist distinction between the classes, according to which the classes which hold property are naturally evil while the "proletariat," the industrial workers, are the Messianic class endowed with every virtue. A derivative of this distinction distinguishes between the capitalist nations which are by nature "imperialistic" and "militaristic" and the innocent "Peoples' Democracies." The tendency to call white black and black white is accentuated and justified by these unreal distinctions. The fury of communist self-righteousness is aggravated furthermore by the Marxist error of equating egotism with the economic motive so that the most powerful oligarch, driven and corrupted by the lust for power, will appear innocent to his own conscience and the delusions of his community because he makes no profit and owns no property.

A third pretension of communism is usually obscured by the stock criticism against Marxism. It is rightly accused of being deterministic, that is, of underestimating the freedom of man and of emphasizing the determined character of his culture and of his convictions, which are said to be rooted in his economic interest. This determinism is at least half true and not nearly as dangerous as a supplementary and contradictory dogma according to which history works toward a climax in which the proletarian class must by a "revolutionary act" intervene in the course of history and thereby change not only history but the whole human situation. For after this act man is no longer both creature and creator of history but purely the creator who "not only proposes but also disposes." This idea involves monstrous claims of both omnipotence and omniscience which support the actual monopoly of power and aggravate its evil. Molotov illustrates the pretensions of omniscience when he declares that the communists, guided by "Marxist-Leninist science," know not only the inner meaning of current events but are able to penetrate the curtain of the future and anticipate its events. This tendency of playing God to human history is the cause for a great deal of communist malignancy. The seemingly opposite tendency to regard men as the product of economic circumstance supports the pretension; for it makes it possible for a group of elite to pretend to be the manipulators of the destiny of their fellow men. The pretension reveals the similarity between the Nazi evil, based upon the pretension of Nietzsche's "superman," who makes his power self-justifying, and this kind of superman whose power is ostensibly justified by the fate which appoints him as the creator of historical destiny. Some of the communist fury is the consequence of the frustration of the communist oligarchs, when they discover history to be more complex than anticipated in their logic and find that opposing forces which are marked for defeat in their apocalypse, show a more stubborn strength and resistance than they anticipated.

The Marxist dogmatism, coupled with its pretensions of scientific rationality is an additional source of evil. The dogmas are the more questionable because the tyrannical organization prevents a re-examination of the dogmas when the facts refute them. Ideally, the presuppositions which govern an inquiry into the facts are more inescapable than a liberal culture supposes. It ostensibly believes in the possibility of empirical inquiry without presuppositions, though it has its own dogmas of the idea of progress and the perfectibility of man, for instance; but it is important to have the freedom to re-examine and to dismiss a presupposition if it is refuted by history. The communist irrationality and dogmatism consists of a rigorous adhesion to dogma in defiance of the facts. In this it differs from Nazi irrationality which relies upon mystic intuitions. The communists test every historical fact with ostensible precision and coolness, but their so-called science looks at the world through the spectacles of inflexible dogma which alters all the facts and creates a confused world picture. The greatest danger of communist policy comes from the fact that the communists do not know what kind of a world they live in, and what their foes are like. Their own rigorous dogma obscures the facts and their tyrannical system prevents, for motives of fear, the various proconsuls of their imperium from apprising the men in the Kremlin of the truth.

The rigor of the communist dogmatism creates an ideological inflexibility, consonant with the monolythic political structure. Significantly the hope inside and outside the party that communist inflexibility would be modified, for instance, by the western traditions of Czechoslovakia or the Confucian traditions of China, proved to be mistaken. Communism has been consistently totalitarian in every political and historical environment. Nothing modifies its evil display of tyranny. The combination of dogmatism and tyranny leads to shocking irrationalities in communist trials, where the victims are made to confess to the most implausible charges. Since the communist dogma allows for no differences of opinion among the elect, every deviation from orthodoxy is not only branded as treason but is attributed to some original sinful social taint. Thus the fallen Czech communist leader Shansky confesses that his alleged "nationalist-Zionist" treason must be attributed to his "bourgeois-nationalist" origin.

It is instructive that the actual monopoly of power accentuates the evil in the ideological pretensions of communism while these pretensions give a spiritual dimension to the evils which flow from a monopoly of power. Thus the evil of communism flows from a combination of political and "spiritual" factors, which prove that the combination of power and pride is responsible for turning the illusory dreams of yesterday into the present nightmare, which disturbs the ease of millions of men in our generation.

4. The Anomaly of European Socialism

WESTERN CONSERVATIVES MAKE much of the fact that both socialism and communism are descended from Marxism and like to suggest that there is no essential difference between the two. But in the words of the late German socialist leader, Kurt Schumacher, "If socialism and communism are brothers, they are brothers like Cain and Abel." More accurately, they are half brothers, socialism having a democratic mother and a Marxist father. From its mother it has inherited its fierce devotion to liberty; but one must admit that its eyes, particularly the blindness of its eyes, are inherited from the father, for its vision is blinded by Marxist dogmatism. Liberal democratic socialism does not hold the inherited dogmas with the same degree of consistency as communism, for the acids of experience have corroded many of the dogmas and have forced socialists to make both explicit and implicit adjustments to the democratic ethos. But in spite of these adjustments socialism is still burdened by an excess baggage of Marxist dogma, and this baggage is frequently a hazard to the success of the free world.

An event in recent German history will illustrate both the loyalty of socialism to democracy and its pathetic habit of hanging on to its Marxist dogmatism. During the early days of our occupation of Germany, the socialists were fiercely contesting a Berlin election against the communists. They understood better than many of the occupying authorities what was at stake in the election. A communist victory would have made the position of the Western Powers untenable in Berlin. But this did not prevent the socialists from making their election appeal in terms of strict Marxist orthodoxy. The Communist Party was branded as the instrument of Russian "imperialism"; the bourgeois parties were called the tools of "Western imperialism"; and the conclusion was that "only the Socialist Party is able to promise the German worker eternal peace and a classless society." This theoretical appeal to a utopian heaven in a situation where it was quite well recognized what practical steps were necessary to stay out of a communist hell is a sad illustration of how much the socialists depend upon Marxist dogma, even in a situation where they are resisting the evil effects of that dogma. It may be relevant to report that Mayor Reuter of Berlin had not yet appeared on the political scene; for this redoubtable democrat is one of the few ex-communists who is able to divest himself of communist illusions without either clinging to residual Marxist errors or embracing alternate conservative illusions.

Yet in the early days after Allied victory the German socialists were led astray by their Marxist dogmas less than most socialists in Western Europe. They were in such close contact with the horrible realities of communism that, whatever their illusions, they could not deny the facts. The French socialists required some years of experience with communist cynicism before they could be freed of the dogma that they must not break "working class solidarity" by entering a government without the communists. This position was doubly ironic because the French socialists really belonged not to the working classes but to the intellectual middle classes. They were in the working class only by the grace of their dogma. The Italian socialists were divided between a pro-communist and an anti-communist faction, a division which prevails to this day and makes the democratic position in Italy the more precarious. But, despite these confusions, the well-laid communist plot for swallowing up the socialist parties in the so-called "socialist unity" parties succeeded nowhere unless it was backed up by the power of the Red Army. In Western Europe the socialists' devotion to democracy has gradually triumphed; yet the socialist parties still cling to their Marxist dogmas with remarkable tenacity, incompatible as those dogmas are with the necessities and ideals of democratic politics and much as the socialists' own experience refutes them. Naturally, such a conflict between dogma and experience is a source of confusion in both domestic and international politics.

The Marxist system rests upon a central dogma which ascribes all historic evil to the institution of property and promises redemption from every ill through the socialization of property. Around this central dogma are clustered a whole series of ancillary and derivative dogmas. One makes a sharp and unreal distinction between the propertied and propertyless classes, the one allegedly evil and the other virtuous. Another makes an equally false distinction between the "capitalist" nations, who are supposedly guilty of the sins of "imperialism" and "nationalism," and the nations who have abolished property and are therefore supposedly innocent. Another dogma asserts the movement of history towards a revolutionary climax in which the balance will be redressed and the weak propertyless masses will triumph over the strong propertied classes. This persuades men to look forward to utopia on the other side of a revolution.

The thesis that "imperialism" is purely the fruit of "capitalism" and that therefore noncapitalist nations are nonimperialistic and internationalist "by definition" has been refuted through the flagrant imperialism of Russia. It is less flagrantly but no less decisively refuted by the contemporary record of the European socialist parties themselves. In the years since the war they have turned out to be excessively nationalistic. They have left the burden of the unification of Europe—whether through the

Schuman Plan, the Strasbourg Assembly, or NATO—to be carried by the centrist Catholic parties, which are despised by good socialists as "reactionary," while the socialists have been either hostile or lukewarm. Their nationalism has been partly due to their supposed immunity from ordinary "nationalistic" traditions and passions, and partly because the various international schemes seemed to them a threat to the scheme of socialization, which was always tantamount to nationalization. A combination of these factors has operated to determine the international policies of both British Labor and German socialism. The French socialists have been a little more cooperative.

The evidence that socialist parties and nations can be guilty of the sins of national pride and lust for power seems not to have invalidated the dogma that derives "nationalism" and "imperialism" from "capitalism" alone. We, as Americans, have good reason to regret the slow rejection of this dogma, for in the minds of Europeans we are the capitalist nation par excellence, and the Marxist dogma operates everywhere—far beyond the confines of communism—to breed anti-American prejudices.

Such well-known anti-communist socialists as the Swedish economist and sociologist, Gunnar Myrdal, and the late Harold Laski, both men with intimate knowledge of the United States, showed by their conclusions about American life that Marxist dogma was at war with empirical knowledge in their minds. The Marxist roots of Bevan's anti-Americanism are apparent. Bevan regards American prosperity as purely the fruit of "exploitation."

He thinks that our "capitalists" want to prepare for war to preserve our economy and will go to war to protect their "markets" in Korea.

The Marxist estimate of the bourgeois ethos is, incidentally, consistently wrong. It pictures the capitalistic classes as spoiling for war in order to "save their profits," but it knows nothing about bourgeois prudential pacifism prompted by fear of the cost of war and resulting taxation.

The Marxist dogma of "imperialism" is as great a hazard today in our fight against communism as it was in the days of our fight with Nazism, because it denies the possibility of making ethical choices between the supposedly common "imperialistic" ends of various "capitalist" states. It is this potent dogma that colors and confuses judgments not only outside the confines of communism but beyond the limits of socialism; it is partly responsible for the "neutralism" of European intellectuals who are not only anti-communists but believe themselves non-Marxist; it colors the attitudes of such diverse intellectuals as the Swiss theologian, Karl Barth (who imagines himself free of all secular ideologies but carries potent prejudices from his Marxist youth), the editor of the English *New Statesman and Nation,* and the intellectuals in the entourage of Prime Minister Nehru.

A nation as strong as ours would be unpopular in any event, both because of the mistakes we make in the use of our power and because of the envy which it arouses among the powerless; but the diffusion of Marxist dogmas and illusions among even non-Marxists in the free world complicates the problem of America's relation to the alliance of free nations. It might be added that the force of the Marxist prejudice is increased by the fact that the realities covered by the concept of "American capitalism" are seen in terms of strict analogy to the tired capitalism of the Continent, particularly that of France.

While the confusion sown by the Marxist dogma is most obvious in international relations, it is also a marked hazard to the success of democracy in domestic politics. Its theory of revolution is incompatible with democratic responsibility; its theory of class conflict does not fit the multiple-class structure of modern industrial societies and is incompatible with the principle of "class collaboration" upon which democratic politics depends; above all, its utopianism interferes with an interest in proximate, rather than ultimate, goals, and that is the point which distinguishes a sane political movement from one that is corrupted by false religious visions. One of the difficulties of socialism in a democratic framework is the inevitable disappointment of these utopian hopes. Even a socialist party which is not consistently Marxist, such as the British Labour Party, is embarrassed by disappointed hopes when it becomes apparent, as indeed it must, that the socialization of property cannot overcome the collective poverty of a nation whose wealth has been destroyed by war; or when it becomes apparent that even after the profits of the coal and steel owners are eliminated, there remain some problems of human relations between workers and authority, now symbolized by the "coal board" and the "steel board." The reaction of Bevan—to look towards a more consistent policy of socialization to overcome present difficulties—reveals him as the leader of a movement towards a stricter Marxist orthodoxy in the heretical Labour Party.

Marxist dogma is, in short, so incompatible with the temper and the necessities of a free society that the question arises why the conservatives' estimate of socialism is not correct; why should it not be regarded as a potential ally of our foe? But this estimate leaves out of account the positive provisional services to democracy of the European socialist parties. Their primary service has been to counter the contrasting *laissez-faire* dogmatism of their conservative critics. Modern conservatism holds that justice is the inevitable fruit of a free play of economic forces, but fails to recognize that, since these forces are never equally balanced, the disproportions of power actually result in grave injustice. The social and political consequences of this miscalculation were precisely the ground in which the seed of the Marxist dogma sprouted. The healthiest Western nations have preserved their economic and political health by following neither the conservative nor the Marxist dogma, but by adopting an empirical wisdom which separates what is true from what is false in each. Thus a political creed which fears the power of the state too much and trusts the automatic balances of the market too uncritically has been balanced by a creed that brings political power to bear upon economic life, though, in its most consistent form, this creed has been too little aware of the peril in a monopoly of political and economic power in the hands of the omnicompetent state.

The confusions occasioned by the dogmatic assumptions of both the Right and the Left prove the validity of President Conant's observation that a high degree of empiricism is a basic requirement for democratic health. All sweeping generalizations and assumptions must be eschewed and the questions must be constantly asked: what is the effect of this or that policy in this or that situation; how well does this particular constellation of power satisfy the requirements of justice and of freedom? A healthy democracy never gives all the power to the proponents of any one dogma; it holds all claims to truth under critical review; it balances all social forces, not in an automatic, but in a contrived harmony of power. In this way it distills a modicum of truth from a conflict of error. That is why the Marxist dogma is robbed of its virulence when it is set in the context of a democratic culture. When its pretensions to wisdom are not supported by a monopoly of power its sweeping generalizations are refuted by daily experience.

Our relations with Europe, and indeed with the whole free world, are complicated by the fact that the illusions spread by the conservative dogma bear exactly the same relation to the wisdom of democratic experience among us as the Marxist illusions bear to the democracy of Europe. We must dare to hope that our common life will become sufficiently integrated to permit common experience to cancel out contrasting dogmas and illusions in international relations as it has in the domestic politics of a free world.

5. The Foreign Policy of American Conservatism and Liberalism

THE REPUBLICAN VICTORY in 1952 returned the Party, which represents the dominant business group in America, to the seats of political power from which it had been excluded for two decades. A part of the reason for its previous failures at the polls is to be found in domestic politics. The American people, having found that the state's sovereign power could be used to establish at least the minimal standards of general welfare, were not disposed to follow the *laissez-faire* policies which dominated the thinking of the business community, particularly not when Roosevelt invented, or adopted from Lord Keynes, a pragmatic version of the policy of state intervention in economic process, which avoided, or seemed to avoid, the perils of a too consistent collectivism.

A part of the reason for the failure of American conservatism must be sought in the field of foreign policy. The two decades, in which it was excluded from power, were in a period in which America was involved in two world wars, was forced to come to terms with the perils of two forms of tyranny; and emerged from the second conflict as incomparably the strongest nation on earth, or at least the strongest of the free nations. American conservatism could not come to terms with hazards and responsibiliites which the growing hegemony of this youthful but powerful nation involved. Except for a small group of conservatives, of which the late Secretary, Henry Stimson, was the best exemplar, American conservatism persisted in an alternation between isolationism, which failed to measure the extent of our peril or the breadth of our responsibilities in the larger world, and a policy of adventurism which failed to judge the limits and hazards to success which even a powerful nation must observe.

This failure of American conservatism in the field of foreign policy is the more remarkable because it is the virtue of traditional European conservatism, to understand the hazards and responsibilities of foreign policy rather better than traditional liberalism. European conservatism is rooted in the aristocratic tradition; and its superior insights are derived in part from long ages of responsibility in this field. It knows the relations of the nations to be governed by power factors, to which the liberal mind is usually oblivious; and it is accustomed to the limited possibilities and short range plans to which the caprices of international relations must reconcile a wise statesman. "Liberalism" of the historic variety is not only inclined to neglect the power factors in a situation but it is prone to project rather more comprehensive plans into the future than the exigencies in international relations warrant.

If American conservatism lacks these virtues, the reason for this defect can be given in one sweeping generalization: American conservatism is not conservative at all in the traditional sense; it is a part of the traditional liberal movement and it exhibits the defects of its creed; but it has not retained many of its virtues. It is not surprising that it should be so. The liberal creed in its various facets is a characteristic of the ethos of the bourgeois class; and was a weapon in its fight against the aristocracy as it sought to disintegrate the old, feudal society in favor of a society in which the individual would have fewer restraints upon his initiative, more flexible and mobile forms of social power and fewer traditional inequalities derived from birth and tradition and irrelevant to present function. As America established its freedom from the aristocratic society by the same historic act in which it established itself as a nation, its orientation is naturally "liberal" *par excellence*. It is a more consistently bourgeois nation than any other and its wide variety of political creeds explicate on the various facets of the liberal ethos in such a way that the term "liberal" has become almost meaningless among us because it is claimed with a measure of validity for the most contradictory programs.

In the political development of America our "conservatives" are conservative only in the sense that they resist innovation and defend the *status quo*. The *status quo*, until the Rooseveltian era, permitted a degree of non-interference by the state in economic process which must make America a paradise for all true devotees of *laissez faire*. The business community, in short, chose, for obvious ideological reasons, to defend that part of the liberal creed which was drawn from the physiocratic theory, and from the philosophy of Adam Smith, and which sought the greatest possible freedom of human initiative from state control particularly in economic activity. This part of the liberal creed also unfortunately made the mistake of identifying human desires with economic ambitions, and of assuming that these and other ambitions were essentially ordinate, that they would be automatically regulated or equilibrated in the market place. This form of liberalism is particularly sympathetic to the business community, both because it protects its economic power from control by the political power and because it corresponds to some characteristic illusions of the businessman, who does not understand the curious compound of forces which go into the making of political power and cohesion; or the dangerous inordinancy of ambition which is exhibited in the realm of politics, particularly in an era of political religions, resulting in demonic political movements. It is characteristic of the business mind that Chamberlain thought that Hitler had a price which reasonable men could meet, and that the typically bourgeois Dutch sought to make themselves safe against Hitler's will-to-power by a meticulous neutrality. When Britain was confronted with great peril, it called Churchill, rooted in an older aristocratic tradition, to the helm. Churchill had two typical virtues in addition to highly unique personal ones, which made him superior to Chamberlain in guiding the destinies of a nation in a catastrophic age. He fully understood the nature of the Nazi demonry. He had no illusions about it being a force with which one could come to terms in some political counterpart of the market place; and he regarded the national and imperial interests in terms of honor and prestige rather than in terms of the "cash nexus."

The American counterparts of Chamberlain were all, or almost all, in the Republican Party. The Republican Party came within one vote of killing an adequate preparedness bill only a short time before we were in the conflict. It consistently underestimated the Nazi peril and consistently challenged the measures of the administration, designed to express our responsibility to the imperiled nations of Europe, when they faced, first the Nazi and then the communist peril. This bourgeois pacifism and isolationism is incidentally a clear refutation of the Marxist thesis that capitalism is inevitably "Imperialistic" and "Militaristic." In a nation with a vast self-sufficient continental economy, some of the Marxist charges are particularly irrelevant, at least when applied to more than the exercise of economic power. The pacifism and isolationism is compounded of a national prudence which does not weigh the factors of interdependence which relate our interests to those of other nations; of blindness to ambitions and lusts among nations which are not contained within the economic motives which prevail in the business world, and to forms of inordinancy in man's collective life which do not come into the category of avarice. The fear of the taxation which war expenditures make necessary, and above all to forms of governmental control which even a conservative and wealthy nation may find advisable in war-time, are additional causes for the pacifism. If Britain turned to an authentic conservative in the hour of peril, our own nation turned to a "liberal" for leadership, when it was apparent that only a small fraction of Republicanism assessed our position, our perils, and our responsibilities correctly. Roosevelt's last two victories at the polls were prompted by the favor he had gained among our citizens, not by his domestic but by his foreign policy. He gained those victories even though the Republican Party advanced candidates from its interventionist wing, partly because the isolationist majority in the Republican Party lacked enthusiasm for its interventionist candidate, and partly because Roosevelt was able to embarrass the candidate with the record of his Party on foreign affairs in Congress. The Republican victory of 1952 was gained with the help of the immense prestige of a General who had been one of the instruments of a Rooseveltian foreign policy. His victory was significantly engineered by eminent proconsuls of the budding American imperium, partly drawn from the Army and partly from business, who had had direct experience with the responsibilities of American power and the hazards of the American position in the world.

What was the basis of the left-of-center "liberalism" as espoused by Roosevelt, and why was it superior to the classical "liberalism" of Republican conservatism in foreign policy? Roosevelt's "liberalism" was the inheritor of those portions of the liberal tradition which emphasized not so much the freedom of economic forces from control as the development of political institutions to accomplish the liberal objectives of universal suffrage, equal rights under the law, minimal standards of welfare and international comity.

In Europe this form of "liberalism" was frequently expounded by Democratic Socialism, leaving the conservative liberalism, interested primarily in free enterprise, to rather pathetic right-wing "Liberal" Parties. In Britain the traditional Liberal Party was destroyed, a part of it finding refuge in the Conservative Party and the greater part of it merging with a rather pragmatic socialism in the Labour Party. In America this liberalism, first expounded by Jefferson, was rendered impotent by the rapid expansion of the frontier and then by the increasing expansion of the American economy, so that the liberalism of Adam Smith seemed to have a particular plausibility among us. Jeffersonianism was also rendered impotent by the identification of the Party of Jefferson with the Southern planters and their subsequent defeat in the Civil War. It did not emerge as a power on the American scene until the days of Wilson, and then of Roosevelt. Naturally the changing circumstances of a highly centralized economy forced the critics of a business civilization to amend the Jeffersonian dictum that the "least possible government is the best," and to engage in pragmatic ventures in political control over economic process which seemed to its critics, at least, to be rank forms of collectivism.

It may seem ironic that a Party which claimed to derive its inspiration from Jefferson should advocate forms of political control which violated the Jefferson dictum about minimal government; but the fact that the similarity between the Jeffersonian dictum and the *laissez-faire* formula did not determine American political alignments, proves that the important element in Jeffersonianism was not the insistence on freedom of the economy from political control, but its critical attitude toward injustices which developed in a commercial civilization. The logic of economic interest was responsible for the paradoxical fact that the spiritual children of Jefferson advocated a state control strong enough to insure justice, while the heirs of Hamilton took up the discarded Jeffersonian dictum.

It was not surprising that the Party under Wilson and Roosevelt gathered all the critics of a business civilization, including, on the one hand, the less favored, recently arrived immigrant groups, and, on the other hand, the intellectual and professional groups who were not impressed by the business ethos, were sensitive about the injustices which developed in a free enterprise economy and were conscious of the nation's responsibility to the world. If the liberalism left-of-center came under the criticism of its foes on the ground that it tolerated or condoned a collectivism, which violated the individualism of traditional liberalism; the liberalism right-of-center could, on the other hand, be accused of frustrating the desire for social change and a broader justice which was also a part of traditional liberalism.

The question is why this left-of-center liberalism was more astute and effective in foreign policy than the liberalism expounded by Republicanism. After all, its moralistic illusions were almost as certain a source of confusion in foreign affairs as the prudential cautions of the conservative liberals. Democratic socialism in both Europe and America was touched by pacifism. The British Labour Party defeated a conscription bill on the April before the outbreak of the war, to the consternation of France. The Scandinavian Socialists prided themselves on the disarmament of their nations and failed to recognize that their security was parasitic on the British Navy. The pacifism and illusionism of Bryan, Wilson's first Secretary of State, are well known. The people in Roosevelt's camp were almost as anxious to preserve the neutrality of the nation for moralistic reasons, as the conservative liberals were for prudential reasons. Labor was almost as isolationist as business, and the pacifism and isolationism of agrarian radicalism, symbolized by Senators Norris and LaFollette, are well known. Perhaps the primary reason for the superiority of the Democratic exponents of liberalism over the Republican exponents in foreign policy must be attributed to the fortuitous circumstance that Democratic Presidents were in power when the nation confronted the perils of the first and the second world wars. The responsibilities of office are a wonderful school for the Party in power; and some of the mentioned distinctions are merely due to the difference between the responsibilities of office and the irresponsibilities of opposition, aggravated by the fact that in the American system the opposition bears no responsibility for formulating alternative policy.

However, there is another potent cause for the superior wisdom of the Rooseveltian type of liberals despite their weakness in foreign policy. These liberals were genuinely "internationalist" in outlook, as opposed to the prudential isolationist nationalism of the Republicans. In the case of Wilson, the internationalist outlook was devoid of appreciation of the power-political elements in international relations, which characterize true conservatism. Roosevelt's realism corrected this fault; but both Roosevelt and Wilson were inclined to defy one of the canons of a wise conservatism which restricts policy to limited and foreseeable ends. They had the penchant of the modern liberal for wide and sweeping objectives. Thus Wilson, who at first saw the first world war as only a trade dispute in which we had no interest, ended by interpreting it as a crusade to "make the world safe for democracy." Among his "principles" of democracy, which was to have the consequence of disorganizing some fairly viable social cohesions, was his idea of "the self-determination of nations." The same

penchant for wide, abstract, and sweeping objectives is
to be noted in the present popularity among American
liberals for abstract projects such as world government.
The similarity under the difference between Roosevelt's
realism and Wilson's "idealism" is illustrated by Roosevelt's efforts to guard against the charge which the Ger-
mans made after the first world war against Wilson. They
accused him of violating the promises implied in his "four-
teen points" in the Versailles Peace Treaty. Roosevelt
sought to prevent a similar charge by the simple expedient
of insisting on "unconditional surrender." This sweeping
correction of Wilson's "idealism" may have prevented an
effective revolution against Hitler's tyranny by destroying
the hope of an effective alternative to the fate to which
Hitler's Germany was doomed. It was in any case too
sweeping a formula to conform to the standards of a pragmatic conservation in foreign policy.

Whatever may have been the causes of the superior
wisdom of Roosevelt's type of liberalism in the realm of
foreign policy, and whatever may have been its residual
weaknesses, he undoubtedly led the nation with great
skill in assuming our responsibilities in a growing world
community, to which it was not accustomed by experience and tradition, and which it was inclined to resent.
Just as men thought that the achievement was a personal
one and that it must be attributed to the political genius
of a single man, Roosevelt died, and a successor, who was
by general consent no political genius, made the hard
decisions required by the peril in which the nation stood

when the ally of yesterday turned out to be as dangerous and as tyrannical a foe as the enemy of yesterday. He was opposed on all of these decisions by American conservatism, which exhibited a continued confusion in the realm of foreign policy by alternating between isolationist irresponsibility, which refused to assert the full strength of America, and adventurous irresponsibility which failed to measure the limits of power which even a powerful nation must observe. Thus our American conservatives have persisted in viewing the vast revolutionary upheavals in Asia, which resulted in the extension of communism there, as merely the consequence of mistakes on the part of our Department of State, and as capable of rectification by rigorous military action on our part. This "illusion of American omnipotence," in the phrase of Dennis Brogan, is a natural mistake of a commercial community which knows that American hegemony is based upon our technical-economic power but does not understand the vast complexities of ethnic loyalties, of social forces in a decaying agrarian world, of the resentments which a mere display of military power creates among those who are not committed to us and who are in any case fearful of the actions of a very powerful nation. If the liberalism of the left has too unqualified confidence in the power of abstract ideas amidst the complexities of international relations, the liberalism of the right trusts pure military power, derived from our economic strength, too much.

We have previously noted that the Eisenhower victory, having reversed political tendencies of two decades, has had the salutary effect of bringing the dominant economic group in the nation into a position of political responsibility. Whatever defects in the outlook of American conservatives may have been due to lack of political responsibility, will thereby be corrected. The danger of the nation embarking upon a long range position of hegemony without the consent of its dominant group will thus be avoided. But it is not yet clear how many errors will be corrected by the responsibilities of office. It is not reassuring that the victory of the President, though due partly to his prestige as a military hero and statesman, was also partly due to promises which seemed particularly designed to satisfy that portion of the victorious Party which had been critical of any policy which was meant to meet the responsibilities of our power in the world; and sometimes the promises, such as tax reduction on the one hand, and a more vigorous policy in Asia on the other hand, seemed as contradictory as the alternation between isolation and adventure in the policies of the Party while it was in opposition.

The passion of the Party for tax reduction and its indecision in regard to commitments in Asia may reveal the same characteristics which led to its failure in previous decades.

If one deprecates the absence of a truly conservative influence in the foreign policy of America, it is not because traditional conservatism is deemed more just or moral. On the contrary, it proved itself wedded to aristocratic interests in domestic policy and it did not rise above national or imperial interests in international affairs. Its virtue consisted chiefly in its ability to gauge factors of power in social and international relations which liberals tended to obscure; and to trust the organic processes of social cohesion rather than the abstract schemes which liberals were inclined to advance. In the words of Ireton, spoken in the Putney debates of Cromwell's army, it trusted in the "rights of Englishmen" rather than in the "rights of man," preferring to enlarge the rights of persons which had already been mutually acknowledged in the actual course of history rather than to grasp after rights which the liberals regarded as "inalienable," but which must remain abstract until they are actually embodied in a living social organism. This instinct for the possible, only a little advanced beyond the actual, instead of the utopian and ideal which hovers so precariously between the possible and the impossible, may be the consequence of experience and responsibility, to be distinguished from the visions of the irresponsible observer. It may also be the fruit of Christian wisdom, which has learned the fragmentariness of all human striving and the measure of egoistic corruption in all human virtue. There may be a larger deposit of Christian wisdom in the traditional communities of Europe than in a nation like ours in which the viewpoints of the Enlightenment won a unique triumph and colored even our Christian inheritance: for a combination of the visions of the Enlightenment and the optimism of sectarian Christianity, developed in the expansive conditions of a nation with an advancing frontier and an expanding economy, have tended to obscure the realities of history and to identify Christianity with pure "idealism" rather than with a sense of responsibility in the actual conditions of human existence.

Our problem, both in foreign policy and in other affairs, is how to generate the wisdom of true conservatism without losing the humane virtues which the liberal movement developed. Ordinarily one associates this conservatism with the man of affairs, as contrasted with the "idealogue." As a "man of affairs," he knows the limits of abstract formulae in the actual web of conflicting interests and values. He is therefore a "pragmatist" by experience. Unfortunately the businessman, as a man of affairs, fails us in the complexities of politics, particularly of foreign politics, because his experience is limited to a type of fairly simple collective endeavor in which the economic motive is isolated from other lusts and ambitions of men. He therefore gains a rather too simple view of human nature. He does this particularly if he is informed by a philosophy which has interpreted human nature in terms of "economic man" and which falsely regards all human striving as essentially ordinate; and all social cross purposes as resolvable in the market place. Furthermore, he is tempted to illusions by the fact that the power which he manipulates is covert, rather than overt; and when it becomes overt there is too simple a transfer from economic to military power. These facts dispose the commercial classes to that puzzling alternation between a pacifism, which obscures the factors of power, and an assertion of power, which is heedless of all the moral and cultural factors in an international situation.

Commercial affairs thus tend to create abstract systems of thought, as distant from the realities of a complex world of politics, and as unrealistic as the systems of the "idealogues" whom the men of affairs tend to despise because they "have never met a payroll." This is just another way of saying what was our thesis in the beginning: that American conservatism is but another version of the liberal creed and that this creed, whatever its virtues, does not come to terms with the realities of either power or interest; and is inclined to elaborate schemes which violate the organic and historical process in the human community.

The other version of the liberal creed, elaborated in America under Roosevelt's leadership, managed, under the pressure of its responsibilities to slough off the illusionary defects, to conceive a domestic policy which managed to strike a fairly tolerable balance between the perils of injustice in an unregulated economy, and the perils of tyranny in too much political control over economic affairs; and in foreign affairs to achieve the wisdom which we have already extolled. One may hope that the victory of the Republican Party will solidify some of these achievements as they can only be solidified when accepted by the Party of the opposition; and that it will give a chance for our men of affairs to add political to economic experience. For the businessmen who have been subjected to this school in our vast American empire (as for instance

John J. McCloy) have proved that they have the resiliency to adapt themselves to the wider and more complex field. Meanwhile, there remains among our intellectuals, particularly among those who vainly try to comprehend the height and depth of human affairs within the confines of the natural sciences, a very real threat to a genuine conservatism.

For the "natural science" approach to political reality is tempted to an alternation between two errors which have dogged the spirit of liberalism: an excessive determinism, which regards the affairs of men in history as determined as those of physical and brute nature, and an excessive voluntarism which presumptuously seeks to manage and manipulate men as nature is manipulated. This voluntarism invariably involves a theory of an elite of managers, of which communism presents us with the most flagrant and dangerous example. It makes the theories of aristocratic societies seem mild by comparison. This type of voluntarism has plans for managing human beings for the sake of directing them to "socially approved" ends. It includes the sociologist who is conducting scientific experiments to determine how the altruistic motives of men can be strengthened and the egoistic impulses weakened. It also includes the anthropologist who proposes scientific breeding in order to eliminate eugenically the present "ape-man" who is not capable of managing affairs in a technical age; and the biologist who thinks that the study of social insects will give us some useful clues for managing the next stage in human evolution; or the group of social scientists who propose a world-wide study of human aggressiveness; or the psychologists who want to study the relation between hunger and racial prejudice; or the educator who proposes a tyrannically controlled system of international education in order to insure the absence of national prejudices from the education; or the political scientist who would organize a world government with power to suppress national interests on the ground that "nationalistic parochialism" has become "criminal" at this stage of human developments. These proposals represent the froth in the brew of American "liberal" culture. But they are rather indicative of the hiatus between the common-sense wisdom which the man in the street and the men of affairs, have acquired for the management of our common life and the pretentious wisdom of the culture of liberalism. If Winston Churchill may be regarded as the best examplar of true conservatism in our day, we might profit from his reaction to this type of academic wisdom. At the Anniversary Convocation of the Massachusetts Institute of Technology, Mr. Churchill declared, "the Dean of the Humanities assured us this morning that the day would soon come when psychologists could control the very thoughts in our minds. I will be well content to be dead in that day."

One may well wonder how the social and psychological sciences which have proved their value on so many levels of human experience, should generate so many naive miscalculations on the ultimate level of political wisdom. Perhaps the miscalculations are the fruits of two errors which characterize all merely naturalistic approaches to the problems of human behavior. It is not understood that the "nature" which is to be mastered and manipulated contains the self, with all of its guile of spirit; and that the mind which is supposed to master nature, is also involved in this same self, with all of the capacities of self-deception. Most of the pretentious analogies between the mastery of natural and of historical evil, are therefore misleading. The common-sense wisdom of the symbolic "man in the street" is therefore usually superior to the more pretentious scientific knowledge of the learned men. That wisdom is derived from an empiricism which does not rest upon the misleading presuppositions of the scientist. It is consequently not tempted to deny or to obscure some very obvious facts about human behavior.

Perhaps it is as useless to define the ideal conservatism as to restore exact meaning to the word liberal. A conservative obviously is interested in conserving something. Usually he is interested in conserving some *status quo*, while the "liberal" is presumably free of the current prejudices which support the *status quo*. In Western history, liberalism as a spirit connotes this freedom but it also connotes a specific creed, associated with the rise of both bouregois life and modern learning. Both the spirit and the creed of liberalism emphasized the value and the dignity of the individual in contrast to traditional forms of culture which did not recognize the individual apart from his social function or position. But in addition the creed of liberalism included some illusions about human nature and human history which have become the source of confusion to our generation. Therefore we must be concerned to preserve most of what is known as the spirit of liberalism, while life refutes the liberal creed. But while we cannot condone the spirit of conservatism, at least insofar as it is an ideological defense of some *status quo* it is necessary to regain that part of the conservative creed, as elaborated in Western, and particularly in British history. This creed emphasized historical rather than abstract modes of social engineering, and recognized the perennial sources of recalcitrance to moral norms in human life. It was therefore intent upon developing politics as the art of the possible, being cautious not to fall into worse forms of injustice in the effort to eliminate old ones. Perhaps the creed of such a conservatism is most adequately expounded in Edmund Burke's *Reflections on the Revolution in France*. This type of conservatism is on the one hand the product of experience, particularly of the type of experience which includes all of the problems of man's collective life rather than merely the economic ones. If we are at all successful in sustaining our political hegemony in the free world we will become the more successful by the accretion of experience. In part, this conservatism is the product of Christian rather than "idealistic" approaches to the perennial facts of human nature. Whether we win it or not therefore depends upon the addition of Christian humility to the compound which must serve us as wisdom. Naturally we will be the more successful if we are not too anxious about the exact political source of this wisdom, whether from the traditional right or the traditional left, whether from the men of reflection or the men of affairs.

6. *Ideology and the Scientific Method*

THE OPINIONS WHICH men and groups hold of each other and the judgments which they pass upon their common problems are notoriously interested and unobjective. The judgments of the market place and the political arena are biased, not only because they are made in the heat of controversy without a careful weighing of evidence, but also because there is no strong inclination to bring all relevant facts into view. While the ideological taint upon all social judgments is most apparent in the practical conflicts of politics, it is equally discernible, upon close scrutiny, in even the most scientific observations of social scientists. The latter may be free of conscious bias or polemic intent. Yet every observer of the human scene is distinguished from the scientific observer of the sequences of nature by the fact that he is, in some sense, an agent in, as well as an observer, of the drama which he records.

The relation of interest to historical knowledge is so obvious and inevitable that it is somewhat surprising that it came fully into view so late in the history of culture, and that Marxism, a polemic creed, should have been the primary agent of its discovery. The Marxist sponsorship of the theory of ideology was unfortunate, for Marxism discredited itself so quickly by becoming the prisoner of its own ideological presuppositions, that it has seemed unnecessary to deal seriously with the Marxist theory. Yet Marxism stumbled upon an important, and in some respects, an insoluable problem, in the realm of historical knowledge.

Despite its limitations we may well begin with the Marxist conception of ideology. According to Marx, even the most "objective" interpretations of human life and destiny, of legal and moral norms and ideals are in fact the rationalization of the interest of the ruling groups of a society, and mirror the economic interests of that group. The charge of the *Communist Manifesto* reads: "You transform into eternal laws of nature and reason the social forms springing from present modes and forms of property. What you see clearly in the case of ancient property, what you admit in the case of feudal property you are of course forbidden to admit in the case of your own form of bourgeois property." The Marxist interpretation of ideology naturally betrays the defects of Marxism as a philosophy and as a polemical political creed. It limits the ideological taint purely to economic interest, whereas it is obvious that any form of interest or passion may color our judgments. There are undoubtedly "male" and "female" ideologies, that is viewpoints which are peculiar to the man or the woman, as illustrated, for instance, in Aeschylus' tragedy in the conflict between Antigone and Creon, rooted in the irreducible differences between male and female perspectives upon political issues. Every race and class, every generation and age, every particular locus of time and place in history can be the root of an ideology in so far as a parochial situation may color a judgment about facts beyond that situation.

The Marxist thesis implies but does not explicitly illumine the fact that an ideological taint upon a judgment implies a true and untainted judgment. One could go further and insist that false judgments depend upon true judgments for their prestige. There can be no counterfeit money without genuine money. This fact reveals an aspect of the human situation which the Marxist theory does not understand. It is significant that men cannot simply claim some desired object as their own without seeking to prove that it is desirable in terms of some general scheme of value. This is the tribute which self-interest must pay to a wider system of interest. The fact that men are under an inner necessity of paying this tribute proves that, while self-interest may be powerful, it is never so powerful as to be able fully to obscure a person's knowledge of and loyalty to a wider system of values than those which have his own desires at the center.

The Marxist theory of ideology is not only incomplete on several important issues. It is contradictory on one of them: that is the degree of conscious dishonesty which is involved in the ideological taint. In the Marxist psychology and in its theory of knowledge, conscious dishonesty is specifically disavowed. "Ideology is a process," declared Engels, "which is carried on in the consciousness of the so-called thinkers, but with a false consciousness. The real driving force which moves it remains unconscious, otherwise it would not be an ideological process." It works with pure conceptual material which it unwittingly takes over as the product of thought and therefore does not investigate its relation to a process further removed from and independent of thought.

Thus conscious dishonesty is explicitly denied in the theory of knowledge; but it is affirmed as explicitly in the Marxist polemic against the class foes of the proletariate. They are consistently accused of conscious dishonesty.

Thus Trotsky speaks of the patent dishonesties of the landlords in the first Russian constituent assembly: "They spoke for the rights of idealism, the interests of culture, the prerogatives of a future assembly. The leader of the heavy industries concluded his speech with a hymn in honor of liberty, equality and fraternity. Where were the metallic baritones of profit, the hoarse bass of land rents, where were they hiding? Only the oversweet tenors of disinterestedness filled the hall. But listen for a moment and how much spleen and vinegar there is under this syrup." They are afraid that the land will be "turned over to the dark semi-illiterate peasant. If in their struggle with this dark muzhik the landlords happen also to be defending their property, it is not for their own sakes, O no, but only afterwards to lay it upon the altar of freedom." This biting scorn for the patent dishonesty in ideological pretension would of course be an equally fitting response to the current propaganda in favor of "peoples' democracies," etc., etc.

There are intricacies in the process of self-deception which are not illumined by these contradictory theories. In any event the tendency to "make the worse appear the better reason," must be regarded as at least quasi-conscious.

The inadequacies of the Marxist theory of ideology are perhaps best revealed by the fact that Marxism could make the theory so completely into a weapon of political struggle and apply it to the foe and not to the self. Having interpreted interest in purely economic terms and having assumed that the corruption of ideas by interest could occur only in a society in which there was a disparity of economic interest, it sought to create a society in which a presumed identity or mutuality of interest would eliminate ideology in human affairs. It was not fortuitous that a tyranny should be generated from these illusions in which men of absolute power should mistreat weak men; and that their cruelties should be obscured by the theory which insists that powerful and weak men have no difference of interest so long as both are propertyless.

It is also not fortuitous that a theory of ideology,

which attributes the taint only to a foe should result in
the most monstrous pretensions of purity of reason for
the self, in contrast to the ideologically corrupted opinion
of the foe. Thus Molotov can draw the contrast: "The
diplomacy of capitalist states is based upon mere expedi-
ency and opportunism. The foreign policy of the Soviet
Union alone, based upon the firm foundation of Marxist-
Leninist science, rises above opportunism and is able to
estimate the international scene not only in the immediate
but in the distant future." These claims of omniscience
incidentally reveal the real pathos of the ideological problem. For the greater the pretension of purity and disinterestedness, the greater the impurity.

But the answers of the liberal world to the problem
of ideology are hardly more adequate than the Marxist
answer, though they are considerably less noxious. Many
modern liberal theories derive their defects from the failure to make a sufficiently sharp distinction between the
natural and the socio-historical sciences between *Natur-
wissenschaft* and *Geisteswissenschaft*. Many think that it
is a fairly simple task to apply the "scientific method" first
perfected in the natural sciences, to the world of historical
events and social judgments, thereby eliminating and cor-
recting ideological distortions.

In his *Man and the Modern World*, Julian Huxley
recognizes that when man studies man "he cannot use
the same methods by which he investigates external nature" for when "he investigates human motives his own
motives are involved." This is not the only difference be-

tween the two types of inquiry but it is an important one. Yet Huxley believes that the difficulty will be overcome rather simply though it will "take generations for the social sciences to work out technics for discounting the errors due to bias." Karl Mannheim thinks he has already perfected a sociological epistemology which will progressively free the scientist from the bias of interest, of time and place by a rigorous analysis of the hidden presuppositions which color his judgments. "Whenever we become aware of a determinant which has dominated us," declares Mannheim, "we remove it from the realm of the unconscious motivation into that of the controllable, calculable, and objectified."[1] Presumably a sufficiently rigorous sociology of knowledge will produce social scientists who have achieved a completely transcendent position over the flux of the history in which they are, as mere human beings, involved.

John Dewey believes that the historical sciences are corrupted by the obvious restraints of political and religious authority, which once restricted the freedom of all scientific inquiry. The battle for the freedom of science, he declares, resulted in a compromise in which "the world including man was cut into two parts. One of them was awarded to natural inquiry under the name of physical science. The other was kept in fee simple by a higher authoritative domain of the moral and spiritual (Church and state)." This compromise resulted in "dumping our actual human problems into the lap of the most immature

[1] *Ideology and Utopia*, p. 169.

of all our modes of knowing politics and ethics." The result is that this division of science "which is potent in
human affairs is not a science at all but an ideological
reflection and rationalization of contentious and contending practical politics."[2]

The assumption that historical knowledge is corrupted because it has not yet been freed from authority
has gained a certain degree of plausibility by the fact
that the only way that the natural sciences can be corrupted is by the imposition of external authority (as for
instance biology in Russia today). But the social and political judgments of politicians and journalists, and for that
matter of the man in the street and of the most scientific
social observer are loaded with ideological presuppositions, which are not derived from any explicit pressure
of authority. Modern democracies are, in fact, frequently
threatened with anarchy by the clash of conflicting ideologies, which an active social science may be able to mitigate but which it cannot abolish.

The question is why the ideological taint should be
so much greater in the field of social judgments than in
the natural sciences and why the application of the "scientific method" should be so much less efficacious in remov-
ing bias. The answer to that question involves a rigorous
examination of the difference between the fields of natural
and social sciences and also the difference in the status
of the observer in each field.

[2]*Commentary*, Oct., '47.

II

a.) In his "Plight of the Social Sciences"[3] Robert MacIver emphasizes the many levels of causation which the social sciences must investigate. Every event in history takes place in a half-dozen or more dimensions—geological, geographic, climatic, psychological, social and personal. This complex causation makes it possible to correlate events plausibly in many different ways, usually tempting the observer to "make the field of one's special interest the inclusive ground in which the causes of all relevant phenomena are to be sought."[4] The infinite variety of causal sequences to which every act and event in history is related makes almost every correlation of causes sufficiently plausible to be immune to compelling challenge. Any social theory therefore has some kinship with the procedures of a Rorschach test, which is more revealing about the state of the patient's mind who makes it than about the inkspots which his imagination interprets in terms of various configurations. Obviously absurd correlations can be ruled out, and flagrant bias can be discovered. But no one can give a scientifically conclusive account, for instance, of the fall of the Roman Empire, or of the reason for the rise of Nazism in Germany or for the differences between British and French democracy, which would compel the rejection of a competing or contrasting interpretation. The conclusions arrived at are

[3]In *Social Causation.*
[4]*Ibid.,* p. 77.

partly determined by the principle of interpretation with
which the inquiry is begun.

b.) There are no simple recurrences in history and
therefore no analogies between sequences in various pe-
riods of history which could compel us to accept a propo-
sition that a given policy in a certain period will have
similar effects as a social policy in another period. It is
only partly true, as Windelband and Rickert have argued,
that history is a realm of unique events as distinguished
from the exact recurrences of the physical world. For
there are cycles, recurrences and analogies in history; if
there were not, there would be no basis for scientific investigation. But endless contingencies supervene upon the
recurrences. In the physical sciences there can be controlled experiments which may be endlessly repeated until
the "right" answer is found, but nothing is exactly repeated in history. Therefore a judgment, for instance, that
some "New Deal" policy in America of the twentieth century will expose our nation to the fate of the Roman Empire, on the ground that the latter was the victim of an
analogous policy, can neither be asserted nor refuted with
certainty. Every reliance upon analogy can be refuted by
emphasis upon variants in the compared historical scenes.
Toynbee's analogy between the medieval situation of East-
ern and Western Christendom and the present conflict between Russia and the West sheds some illumination upon
the scene; but not too much. For there are too many novel
factors in the contemporary situation which do not fit
into the analogy.

Aristotle had an understanding of the contingent elements in history and he therefore regarded the analysis of the variables as the domain of *phronesis* rather than *nous*, that is of practical wisdom rather than reason. Yet Aristotle could have a greater degree of confidence than we in the scientific element in historical analysis because he believed in an historical, as well as a natural cycle of recurrence in which the historical norm was revealed. "Among men at least," he declared, "though not among the Gods, though some things are by nature, all are subject to variation. Yet in spite of their variability we may distinguish between what is natural and what is not. How do we distinguish between what is by nature and what by agreement only? In the same way as the distinctions are drawn in other spheres. Thus the right hand is naturally stronger but any man may be ambidextrous. Similarly rules of justice which are not natural but human are not everywhere identical but everywhere there is one constitution marked by nature as the best."[5] Thus, in common with all classical rationalism, he finds normative structures in history analogous to the norms in nature. The modern understanding of the endless possibilities of variation in history makes this basis of historical science invalid. At least it has become obvious that it is not easy to make simple distinctions between the natural and the unnatural, the constant and the variable in historical studies.

c.) Modern historical and social sciences have sought

[5]*Nich. Ethics,* V, 7.

to gain firm ground under their feet by the strategy of interpreting the emergence of novelty in history as subject to discernible patterns, analogous to evolution in nature. There are undoubtedly patterns of historical development, but the analysis of such patterns is subject to hazardous attributions of particular events as causes of subsequent occurrences. These attributions are hazardous not only because of the complexity of the causal chain but because human agents are themselves causes within the causal nexus. The unpredictability of the action of a human agent's action in a particular situation makes prediction of future events highly speculative, and our lack of knowledge of the inner motives of the agents, of past actions renders even analyses of past events very uncertain. If we hazard guesses about the unconscious as well as the conscious motives and incentives of the human agents we make our conclusions even more problematic. Only one historian, Burckhardt, of the recent past predicted anything like the rise of totalitarianism. It might be claimed that the ability to predict consequences of given events and actions is the real criterion of the adequacy of scientific procedures. Without conclusive predictions the refutation of ideologically-tainted political policies becomes practically impossible; for every political argument involves and implies a prediction that the desired policy will redound to the general welfare. Refutation of such a claim would have to offer indisputable proof that the prediction is false. The proof would have to depend upon exact analogies between past and future events.

Such proof is impossible. Thus recently the gas-producing states sought legislation which would have prevented government control of the gas, piped from producer to consumer states. Regulation was thought desirable because ordinary competitive processes would not operate to hold prices down. The oil producing states argued that competition between various types of fuel would serve the purpose of regulating prices. Economists generally held this thesis to be highly improbable; but it was sufficiently plausible to be the ideological garment by which naked interest could be covered. There was no indisputable evidence on how competition between various types of fuel would affect the market.

If it is difficult, if not impossible, to refute conclusively flagrant forms of ideology which operate in ordinary political polemics, it is even more difficult to come to terms with the subtler ideologies which lie at the basis of the ethos of a whole age or culture. Consider the concept of "economic man" as elaborated in classical economics. Morris Cohen, despite a skeptical attitude toward the scientific elements in the social sciences, thinks that the concept of "economic man" is no more hazardous an abstraction than any generalization in the physical sciences. Yet the concept is clearly an "ideology" of a rising bourgeois class. It embodies the individualistic prejudices and illusions of that class, by underestimating the ethnic, national, traditional and other social ties which might prevent an individual from seeking his economic advantage in complete freedom as an individual. It furthermore overemphasizes the economic motive as the key to mystery of human incentives and obscures such motives as the desire for security, for social prestige and approval, and the desire for power. Some of these mistakes have been corrected, but not so much by a more astute science as by subsequent history which proved the bourgeois interpretation of human incentives to be inadequate. This subsequent history could not have been anticipated by the most enlightened social analysis, in so far as it was intimately and organically involved in the peculiar prejudices of its age.

d.) Judgments in the field of history are ultimately value judgments in the sense that they do not intend merely to designate the actions which lead to desired ends but that they seek to give guidance on the desirability of ends. Since history moves above the level of natural necessity and involves actions which seek ends in a wider realm of meaning, the ultimate question about an action or policy is the ethical one: whether the end is desirable. Even the skeptics who try to reduce the concept of desirability to that of "the desired" must admit that human beings have a remarkable penchant for masking what they desire under the idea of the desirable. Indeed, as we have already had occasion to observe, it is the very nature of ideology to confuse the two, not because they are identical but because of the desirability or "value" of an end is necessary to sanction the fact that it is desired.

The question is in what degree the scientific method can unmask precisely this tendency to pretend a wider value for an act than merely its gratification of the desires of the agent. The scientific method is obviously most potent when we limit the question to specific and narrow ends and ask what is desirable to achieve the end of health, or security, or the national interest, or the preservation of civilization. But every specific end is enmeshed in a vast system of ends and means; and we cannot ascertain the desirability of an immediate end without making value judgments about the total schemes of meaning in which such judgments are made or by which they are informed.

We cannot criticize these total schemes of meaning scientifically for every scientific procedure presupposes them. If metaphysics is, as Collingwood claims, the analysis of the presuppositions of our sciences, we can come to terms with the adequacy of the total structure of meaning by metaphysical analyses. The scientific method may help us in detecting an ideological taint in which some partial and parochial interest is sanctified by the prestige of the whole value scheme. Let us take the ideological conflict in modern technical society as an illustration. Even where the liberal world is not subject to the Marxist challenge, there is an ideological conflict between the more favored and the less favored members of the community. It is to be noted that in the more healthy societies this conflict does not result in a disruption of the community because it takes place against the background of value systems which do rough justice to both the individual and social dimension of human existence. But the degree to which individuality and individual initiative is cherished on the one hand, and social solidarity and security on the other, is clearly ideological. The bourgeois community tends to be libertarian and the industrial workers tend, even when they are not Marxist, to be equalitarian and collectivist. In this situation it is interesting to note what social science can and cannot do. A careful analysis of social sequences and causalities can refute the more extravagant claims of each side. There is, for instance, a pretty conclusive evidence that an uncontrolled economy does not automatically make for justice, and that a compounding of political and economic power, according to collectivist programs, will threaten both justice and liberty. Those societies in which there is a relative degree of impartial social observation mitigate the ideological conflict, but they cannot eliminate it. They are powerless to do so because of the existential intimacy between interest and idea. The classes which prefer liberty to security are those which already have a high measure of security through their social and professional skills, and who do not like to have their economic power subjected to political power. The classes on the other hand which prefer security to liberty are on the whole devoid of special skills and therefore individual securities; and are exposed to the perils of a highly integrated technical society, and therefore fear insecurity more than they fear the loss of liberty. There can be no scientific dissolution of these preferences. It is probably true that the health of a democratic society depends more upon the spirit of forbearance with which each side tolerates the irreducible ideological preferences of the other than upon some supposed scientific resolution of them, because the scientific resolution always involves the peril that one side or the other will state its preferences as if they were scientifically validated value judgments.

The field of historical events thus differs radically from the field of natural events in the complexity of the causal chain and by the fact that human agents intervene unpredictably in the course of events. These two factors prevent any scientific method from leading to absolutely compelling conclusions, because all alternative conclusions can always be plausibly presented.

III

There is, however, an even more marked difference between the status of the observer of the realm of nature and the realm of history. The scientific observer of the realm of nature is in a sense naturally and inevitably disinterested. At least, nothing in the natural scene can arouse his bias. Furthermore, he stands completely outside of the natural so that his mind, whatever his limitations, approximates pure mind. The observer of the realm of history cannot be disinterested in the same way, for two reasons: First, he must look at history from some locus in history; secondly, he is to a certain degree engaged in its ideological conflicts. This engagement is most obvious in the case of a statesman who is a proponent of a particular interest of class, race, or nation, but it is also obvious in the case of a more impartial social scientist. "Knowledge," declares Professor George Adams, "is the achievement of a spectator who stands outside the scene which he interprets. To achieve this the mind must emancipate itself from the circumstances to which it owes its birth and transcend the limitations of its own bias."[6] If this be the requirement of historical knowledge it is so severe that it can only be approximated. Furthermore, the challenge to transcend the limits of its own bias is in a sense a moral rather than an intellectual one. That is to say, it is addressed to the self rather than to the mind, i.e., to a self or to a will which is able to use intellectual processes to justify its own ends. Thus we arrive once more at the problem which was obscured rather than illumined by the Marxist theory of ideology, the problem of the conscious element in social and historical bias. "What a man had rather believe," declared Francis Bacon, "he will more readily believe,"[7] thus calling attention to the existential intimacy between idea and interest in human affairs. The observers of history are selves rather than minds because their interest and their will is more immediately engaged than in the observation of nature. The further they are removed in time or in space from an historical encounter the more they can become pure mind, that is, the more they can scientifically analyze without the corruption of passion and interest. Thus the field of historical observation presents us with infinite

[6]*Ethical Principles of the New Civilization,* a symposium edited by Ruth Anshen.

[7]*Novum Organum,* 67, 49.

grades of engagement from the obvious engagement of
the practical statesman through the observations of social
scientists who stand upon some contemporary ground of
impartiality to the observations of social and historical
scientists of a subsequent age who have gained a perspec-
tive in time upon the scene of conflict between various
interests and passions. These various shades of engagement also determine the degree to which selves rather
than minds must be appealed to. If it is a self rather than
a mind, no scientific method can compel a self to cease
from engaging in whatever rationalization of interest may
seem plausible to it. It is for this reason that we must not,
on the one hand, ever despair of an adequate scientific
method mitigating ideological conflicts in history, but
must, on the other hand, recognize the limits of its power.
Perhaps an illustration taken from current politics will
illustrate both the possibilities and the limits. In a dispute
on the wages of steel workers it was obviously valuable to
have a Wage Stabilization Board sufficiently impartial to
render an opinion of relative impartiality on the dispute,
but it was also inevitable that one side should challenge
the impartiality of its findings so that they became again
a part of the dispute. No perfection of method can thus
completely overcome ideological conflict.

The field of historical events is too complex and too
lacking in exact analogies in its recurrences to coerce the
mind to a particular interpretation of the causal sequences,
but, even if the mind could be coerced, the historical observer may always turn out in the end to be an agent

in history rather than an observer of it, with a sufficient stake in the contests of history to defy conclusions which should compel the mind but will not compel the interested self.

7. *Democracy, Secularism, and Christianity*

FOR A LONG time a debate has been waged between Christian and secular leaders on the question whether democracy is the product of the Christian faith or of a secular culture. The debate has been inconclusive because, as a matter of history, both Christian and secular forces were involved in establishing the political institutions of democracy; and the cultural resources of modern free societies are jointly furnished by both Christianity and modern secularism. Furthermore there are traditional non-democratic Christian cultures to the right of free societies which prove that the Christian faith does not inevitably yield democratic historical frutis. And there are totalitarian regimes to the left of free societies which prove that secular

95

doctrine can, under certain circumstances, furnish grist for the mills of modern tyrannies. The debate is, in short, inconclusive because the evidence for each position is mixed.

Perhaps a fair appraisal of it would lead to the conclusion that free societies are the fortunate products of the confluence of Christian and secular forces. This may be so because democracy requires, on the one hand, a view of man which forbids using him merely as an instrument of a political program or social process. This view the Christian and Jewish faiths have supplied. On the other hand, a free society requires that human ends and ambition, social forces and political powers be judged soberly and critically in order that the false sanctities and idolatries of both traditional societies and modern tyrannies be avoided. This sober and critical view is the fruit both of some types of Christianity and of the secular temper with its interest in efficient causes and in immediate, rather than ultimate, ends.

Democracy as a political institution is rooted in the principle of universal suffrage; which arms every citizen with political power and the chance to veto the actions of his rulers. It implements the thesis that governments derive their authority from the consent of the governed. Both clerical absolutism and orthodox Protestantism's principle of the divine rights of kings had to be challenged before political democracy could arise. As a matter of history the later Calvinism and the Christian sects of the seventeenth century and the rationalism of the eighteenth century, equally contributed to the challenge of religiously sanctified political authority. In our own nation, the equal contributions which were made to our political thought by New England Calvinism and Jeffersonian deism are symbolic of this confluence of Christianity and secularism in our democracy.

There is no doubt that the economic institutions of a free society rest upon secular theories and, moreover, upon some erroneous ones. What is usually now defined as "free enterprise" is a form of economic organization which rests upon a physiocratic theory, which is consistently secular and naturalistic. It erroneously assumes that the ambitions of men are contained within the bounds of what is called "nature"; it erroneously believes that the desires of men are chiefly economic and essentially ordinate and that the market place is a sufficient instrument for the coordination of all spontaneous human activities. These are grievous errors. Some of them, being introduced into history at the precise moment when a technical civilization transmuted the static inequalities into dynamic ones, led to the early injustices of modern industrialism. But none of the errors could prevent the classical economic theory from rendering two great services to the development of a free society.

The one was to encourage the coordination of mutual services without political coercion, thereby establishing the flexibility of a democratic society. This contribution remains even after most healthy democracies have discovered that the market place is not an adequate coordinator, and have supplemented the automatic harmonies of interest with various forms of contrived balances in which the political power plays a role.

The other was to make genuinely secular (that is, non-sacred) objects and ends of human striving morally respectable. A free society encourages a multitude of activities which are not in themselves sacred; and it discourages the premature sanctities in which both traditional societies and modern forms of collectivism abound; partly because they make some center of political power into a false center of meaning. It must be noted, of course, that an explicit secularism disavowing reverence for the holy, and interest in the ultimate, may generate many false sanctities and idolatries. The idolatries of democracy, the worship of efficiency and the self-worship of the individual are religiously banal but comparatively harmless compared with the noxious idolatries of modern secular totalitarianism. The latter prove that an explicit denial of the ultimate and divine may be the basis for a religious politics which generates idolatries. On the other hand, the Reformation's principle of the sanctity of all work contributed to the vigor of a free society by giving men the assurance of serving God in ordinary, that is in secular, callings.

The ethos of a free society is even more problematical than its political and economic institutions. Obviously a democratic society requires a respect for the individual which will prevent him from being made into a mere instrument of a social or political process, and which will guard his integrity against collective power. Modern secular thought prides itself upon the idea that its optimistic view of human nature, depending upon an erroneous identification of the virtue and the dignity of man, laid the foundation of modern democracy. This is true only in the sense that a too pessimistic view of human nature, whether of a Hobbes or of a Luther, may lead to political absolutism. Democracy does indeed require some confidence in man's natural capacity for justice. But its institutions can be more easily justified as bulwarks against injustice. Indeed it is because democracy holds every public power under public scrutiny and challenges every pretension of wisdom, and balances every force with a countervailing force, that some of the injustices which characterize traditional societies, and modern tyrannies, are prevented.

Christian thought is offended by the idea that secularism is an aid in delivering traditional societies from their idolatries. Ostensibly the worship of the true God eliminates reverence for false sanctities. But Christians cannot deny that the religious theory of divine right of kings has been a powerful force in traditional societies; nor must they obscure the fact that even a true religion frequently generates false identifications of some human interest with God's will. Secularism is offended by the charge of its affinity with totalitarianism. There are in fact two secular theories of the community and only one of them obviously makes for totalitarianism; the one theory, the thesis of classical economics, was held by the middle classes. The Marxist theory was the weapon of the industrial classes. They both make faulty analysis of the human situation. But the classical theory provides for a multiplicity of powers and the Marxist theory leads to a monopoly of power. All the errors of the first theory are partially relieved by its one virtue; and all the truth in the second theory does not redeem it from this one serious error. The history of our age has no more significant development than that the uneasy conscience of sensitive spirits about the injustices which arose from disproportions of power in a liberal society have been overcome by the fact that the alternative organization of society, when carried through consistently, leads to a monopoly of power; and a monopoly of power leads to all the evils which the Russian tyranny exhibits. The so-called left opinion, whether Christian or secular, must plead guilty to its failure to foresee the perils of this development. Modern conservative opinion is mistaken, however, in insisting that an appreciation of the role of political power must lead to the monopoly of power of which the end product is tyranny. For the healthiest democracies have taken steps both to prevent the partial monopoly of economic power which obtained in the early organization of liberal society and to ward off total monopoly of economic and political power which results from a consistent application of the Marxist theory. Meanwhile the facts about human nature which make a monopoly of power dangerous and a balance of power desirable are understoood in neither theory but are understood from the standpoint of the Christian faith.

The democratic wisdom which learns how to avoid and negate conflicting ideologies, based upon interest, may be, of course, the result of experience rather than of special Christian insights. But it cannot be denied that biblical faith (from which Judaism and Christianity are derived) is unique in offering three insights into the human situation which are indispensable to democracy. The first is that it assumes a source of authority from the standpoint of which the individual may defy the authorities of this world. ("We must obey God rather than man.") The second is an appreciation of the unique worth of the individual which makes it wrong to fit him into any political program as a mere instrument. A scientific humanism frequently offends the dignity of man, which it ostensibly extols, by regarding human beings as subject to manipulation and as mere instruments of some "socially approved" ends. It is this tendency of a scientific age which establishes its affinity with totalitarianism, and justifies the charge that a scientific humanism is harmless only because there is not a political program to give the elite, which its theories invariably presuppose, a monopoly of power. The third insight is the biblical insistence that the same radical freedom which makes man creative also makes him potentially destructive and dangerous, that the dignity of man and the misery of man therefore have the same root. This insight is the basis of all political realism in which secular theory, whether liberal or Marxist, is defective; it justifies the institutions of democracy more surely than any sentimentality about man, whether liberal or radical.

The simple fact is that philosophies, whether naturalistic or idealistic, fail to understand man in so far as they try to fit him into a system. The system obscures the height of his spirit, the uniqueness of his being, and the egoistic corruption of his freedom. That is why the dramatic-historical approach to human and divine reality validates itself despite the prestige of modern science. A scientific culture, despite its great achievements, exhibits a curious naivete in surveying the human scene. That is probably due to the fact that mysteries of good and evil in human nature are obscured to those who insist upon making man an object of scientific investigation and try to fit his radical freedom into some kind of system.

It will be seen that the evidence is too complex to justify either the thesis that secularism leads to totalitarianism or the contradictory idea that it is indispensable for the rise and preservation of democracy. One of the significant facts in the history of democracy as in modern history, generally, is that truth seems so often to have ridden into view on the back of error. Perhaps that is how "God maketh the wrath of man to praise Him."

It goes without saying, that democracy is not the sole or final criterion of the adequacy of a culture or truth of a religion. Catholicism, for instance, which is not productive of democratic cultures, at least not unaided, has some graces of the spirit which must be appreciated despite its lacks in relation to democracy. Secular democratic societies, on the other hand, may preserve freedom and sink into phillistinism in their preoccupation with the gadgets and goods of life. But there is a strong affinity at one point between democracy and Christianity: the toleration which democracy requires is difficult to maintain without Christian humility; and the challenges to pretensions of every kind which are furnished in the give and take of democratic life, are, on the other hand, strong external supports for the Christian grace of humility which recognizes the partial and particular character of everyone's interest and the fragmentary character of every human virtue.

8. *The Christian Witness in the Social and National Order*[1]

THE NATURAL INCLINATION of the convinced Christian, when viewing the tragic realities of our contemporary world, is to bear witness to the truth in Christ against the secular substitutes for the Christian faith which failed to anticipate, and which may have helped to create the tragic world in which we now live. Did they not destroy the sense of a divine sovereignty to which we are all subject? And did they not invent schemes of redemption from evil which made repentance unnecessary?

This inclination may also define our responsibility. But I doubt whether it is our primary responsibility. It is also our opportunity to bring the truth of the Word of

---

[1]The substance of this chapter was originally given as an address before the First General Assembly of the World Council of Churches in Amsterdam in the summer of 1948.

God to bear upon the secular roots of our present predicament because our current history is actually a remarkable
illustration of the way Nemesis overtakes the pride of man
and how divine judgment is visited upon men and nations
who exalt themselves above measure.

The liberal part of our culture thought that the Christian idea of the sinfulness of all men was outmoded. In
its place it put the idea of a harmless egotism, rendered
innocuous either by a prudent self-interest or by a balance
of all social forces which would transmute the selfishness
of all into a higher social harmony. The vanity of that
idea was proved by the ever more dynamic disproportions
of power in our society and the ever greater destruction
of community in a technical society. Sometimes the liberal
part of our culture conceived the idea of redemption
through growth and development. Men suffered (so it was
argued) not from sin but from impotence. But fortunately
the whole historical process was itself redemptive. It trans-
lated man from impotence to power, from ignorance to
intelligence, from being the victim to becoming the master
of historical destiny. This illusion proved as tragic as the
first one. Since the sin of man lies in the corruption of
his will and not in his weakness, the possibilities of evil
grow with the development of the very freedom and
power which were supposed to emancipate man.

The obvious illusions of the liberal world prompted
a Marxist rebellion against the whole liberal culture. In
place of confidence in a simple harmony of all social forces
it proclaimed confidence in a new harmony of society

through a revolutionary destruction of property, thus making a social institution the root of evil in man and promising redemption through its destruction. In place of the idea of redemption through endless growth and development it promised redemption through the death of an old order and the rise of a new one. But this was not redemption through the perpetual dying to self of the Christian Gospel. It was the promise of a new life for us through the death of our foes.

The tragedy of our age has been deepened by the fact that 1) this alternative to secular liberalism proved in many respects even more illusory and erroneous, 2) the two forms of error have involved the world in a bitter civil war which rends society asunder from the national to the international community.

It proved even more erroneous because the prophets of this new religion turned into tyrannical priest-kings who, having lost all sense of the contingent character of all human interests and ideas, filled the world with the cruelty of their self-righteousness. It proved more erroneous because the doctrine of the socialization of property when raised to a doctrine of religious redemption, rather than followed pragmatically, merely combines economic and political power in the hands of one oligarchy and produces tyranny. The obvious evils and cruelties of this alternative have given the proponents of the old order good pretexts for not repenting of their own sins but to be content with calling attention to the perils of the alternative.

Perhaps it is because there is a little truth and so much error in both secular alternatives to the Christian faith that they have involved the world in such a hopeless civil war in which each side had enough truth to preserve its sense of high mission and enough error to frighten the other side with the possible consequences of its victory.

We must undoubtedly bear witness against both types of secular illusion from the standpoint of the truth which we have not of ourselves but from the Gospel. In such a witness the contemporary situation offers the Gospel truth a powerful support. We must preach the Gospel in the day in which the modern man who was so confident that he could control his own destiny is hopelessly caught in an historic fate in which the human will seems to have become completely impotent and frustrated. The vaunted virtues of each side are vices from the standpoint of the other side and sins in the sight of God. The word of the Psalmist fits our situation exactly: "The heathen have raged and the people have imagined vain things. But he who sitteth in the heavens shall laugh."

But let us not presume to laugh with God. God's derisive laughter is the justified divine judgment upon this new and yet very old pride of modern man. We must not laugh, lest we forget that His judgment is upon us, as well as upon them. We are too deeply implicated in the disaster of our day to permit ourselves more than provisional testimony against a so-called secular society. That society in both its liberal and Marxist variety came into being, partly because of the deep involvement of Christianity in the social sins of our day and in the stubbornness of the social injustices. A brief catalog of the sins of the Church proves the depth of our involvement. 1) There is no social evil, no form of injustice whether of the feudal or the capitalist order which has not been sanctified in some way or other by religious sentiment and thereby rendered more impervious to change. In a sense the word of Marx is true: "The beginning of all criticism is the criticism of religion. For it is on this ultimate level that the pretensions of men reach their most absurd form. The final sin is always committed in the name of religion." 2) A part of the Church, fearing involvement in the ambiguities of politics, has declared the problems of politics to be irrelevant to the Christian life. It has abandoned modern men in the perplexities of the modern community and has seen brotherhood destroyed in a technical society without a qualm. Usually this neutrality has not even been honestly neutral. The neutral Church is usually an ally of the established social forces. 3) A part of the Church, facing the complexities of the political order, has been content with an insufferable sentimentality. These problems would not arise, it has declared, if only men would love one another. It has insisted that the law of love is a simple possibility when every experience proves that the real problem of our existence lies in the fact that we ought to love one another, but do not. And how do we establish tolerable community in view of the fact that all men, including Christians, are inclined to take advantage of each other? Even now many Christians fatuously hope that Christian conference will speak some simple moral word which will resolve by love the tragic conflict in the world community. The most opportunistic statesman, who recognizes the complexities which this sentimentality obscures, is a publican who may enter the Kingdom of God before the Phariseeism which imagines that we can lift ourselves above the tragic moral ambiguities of our existence by a simple act of the will. 4) A part of the Church, conscious of these perplexities, has been ready to elaborate detailed schemes of justice and of law for the regulation of the political and social life of mankind, below the level of love and of grace. But it has involved itself in a graceless and inflexible legalism. It does not know that all law can easily be the instrument of sin; that inflexible propositions of justice, particularly in the rapidly shifting circumstances of modern technical development, may hinder rather than help the achievement of true justice. One contribution which Christianity certainly ought to make to the problem of political justice is to set all propositions of justice under the law of love, resolving the fruitless debate between pragmatists and legalists and creating the freedom and maneuverability necessary to achieve a tolerable accord between men and nations in ever more complex human relations. We need a pragmatic attitude toward every institution of property and of government, recognizing that none of them are as sacrosanct as some supposedly Christian or secular system of law has made them, that all of them are subject to corruption and that their abolition is also subject to corruption. This freedom need not degenerate into lawlessness, if it is held in the knowledge that "all things are yours, and ye are Christ's and Christ is God's."

We have spoken negatively. The Christian Church must bear witness against every form of pride and vainglory, whether in the secular or in the Christian culture, and be particularly intent upon our own sins lest we make Christ the judge of the other but not of ourselves. But the experience of repentance does not stand alone. It is a part of a total experience of redemption. Positively our task is to present the Gospel of redemption in Christ to nations as well as to individuals. According to our faith we are always involved in sin and in death because we try too desperately to live, to preserve our pride, to maintain our prestige. Yet it is possible to live truly if we die to self, if the vainglory of man is broken by divine judgment that life may be truly reformed by divine grace. This promise of new life is for individuals; yet who can deny its relevance for nations and empires, for civilizations and cultures also, even though these collective forms of life do not have the exact integrity of the individual soul; nor do they have as direct an access to divine judgment and grace?

The situation in the collective life of mankind today is that we have made shipwreck of our common life through the new powers and freedom which a technical civilization has placed at our disposal. The shipwreck, manifested in the misery and insecurity of the whole

world, is an objective historical judgment. It is the death
which has followed upon a vainglorious life of the nations.
Without faith it is nothing but death. Without faith it
generates the sorrow of the world, which is despair. Without faith this confusion is the mark of meaninglessness
which follows the destruction of the simple systems of
life's meaning which have had ourselves, our nation and
our culture at its center. It is by faith in the God revealed
in One who died and rose again that death can become
the basis of new life, that meaninglessness turns into
meaning, that judgment is experienced as grace. Our business is so to mediate the divine judgment and grace that
nations, classes, states and cultures, as well as individuals,
may discern the divine author of their wounds, that they
may also know the possibility of a new and whole life. In
a day of complacency and security the Christian Church
must anticipate the judgment which is to come and declare that the day of the Lord will be darkness and not
light. In the day of judgment and catastrophe the Christian Gospel has a message of hope for those who truly
repent.

It is true that the human situation is such that repentance is always required even as evil always flourishes.
But it is wrong to preach this Gospel *sub specie aeterni-
tatis* as if there were no history with its time and seasons,
and with its particular occasions. Nor is our preaching of
any avail if we only persuade men and nations to acknowledge the original sin which infects us all but not the particular sins of which we are guilty. Not the least of our

tasks is to expound a judgment and a mercy which tempers the wind to the shorn sheep. Must we not warn victorious nations that they are wrong in regarding their victory as a proof of their virtue, lest they engulf the world in a new chain of evil by their vindictiveness, which is nothing else than the fury of their self-righteousness? And is our word to the defeated nations not of a different order, reminding them that their warfare is accomplished seeing that they have received at the Lord's hand double for all their sins, and that the punishment is really at the Lord's hand even though it is not nicely proportioned to the evil committed? Must we not warn powerful and secure nations and classes that they have an idolatrous idea of their own importance and that as surely as they say, "I sit as a queen and shall never know sorrow," so surely shall "in one moment her sorrow come?" And must we not remind those who are weak and defrauded and despised that God will avenge the cruelties from which they suffer but will also not bear the cruel resentment which corrupts their hearts? Must we not say to the rich and secure classes of society that their vaunted devotion to the laws and structures of society which guarantee their privileges is tainted with self-interest; and must we not say to the poor that their dream of a propertyless society of perfect justice turns into a nightmare of new injustice because it is based only upon the recognition of the sin which the other commits and knows nothing of the sin which the poor man commits when he is no longer poor but has become a commissar? Everywhere life is delivered unto death because it is ensnared in self-delusion and practices every evasion rather than meet the true God. And everywhere the Church is caught in this dance of death because it allows the accents of national pride and of racial prejudice, the notes of self-esteem and complacency to color its message, so that the whole business of religion in our day could seem to the cynical observer (even as it must appear to the righteous God) as a vast effort to lobby in the courts of the Almighty to gain a special advantage for our cause in the divine adjudication. If the slogan that the Church should be the Church is to have a meaning other than its withdrawal from the world, must it not mean that by prayer and fasting it has at least extricated itself in some degree from its embarrassing alliances with this or that class, race and nation so that it may speak the word of God more purely, and more forthrightly to each man and nation, but also to each generation according to the peculiar needs of the person and the hour?

A new life is possible for those who die to the old self, whether nations or individuals, at any time and in any situation. But on the positive side there are also special words to be spoken to an age beside timeless words. The new life which we require collectively in our age is a community wide enough to make the world-wide interdependence of nations in a technical age sufferable; and a justice carefully enough balanced to make the dynamic forces of a technical society yield a tolerable justice rather than an alternation of intolerable anarchy and intolerable

tyranny. To accomplish this purpose some of our own preconceptions must go and the same law of love which is
no simple possibility for man or society must be enthroned
as yet the final standard of every institution, structure
and system of justice. To those who exalt freedom we
must declare that freedom without community is not love
but leads to man making himself his own end. To those
who exalt community we must declare that no historic
community deserves the final devotion of man, since his
stature and structure is such that only God can be the
end of his life. Against those who make the state sacrosanct we must insist that the state is always tempted
to set its majesty in rebellious opposition to the divine
majesty. To those who fear the extension of the state for
the regulation of modern economic life we must point
out that their fears are frequently prompted not by a concern for justice but by a jealous desire to maintain their
own power. A tolerable community under modern conditions cannot be easily established; it can be established
at all only if much of what has been regarded as absolute
is recognized to be relative; and if everywhere men seek
to separate the precious from the vile and sharply distinguish between their interests and the demands which
God and the neighbor make upon them.

Perhaps our generation will fail. Perhaps we lack the
humility and charity for the task. There are ominous signs
of our possible and even probable failure. There is the
promise of a new life for men and nations in the Gospel;
but there is no guarantee of historic success. There is no

way of transmuting the Christian Gospel into a system of historical optimism. The final victory over man's disorder is God's and not ours; but we do have responsibility for proximate victories. Christian life without a high sense of responsibility for the health of our communities, our nations and our cultures degenerates into an intolerable other-worldliness. We can neither renounce this earthly home of ours nor yet claim that its victories and defeats give the final meaning to our existence.

Jesus wept over Jerusalem and regretted that it did not know the things that belonged to its peace. In the Old Testament we have the touching story of Abraham bargaining with God about the size of the saving remnant which would be needed to redeem the city. Would fifty or forty or thirty be required? He and the Lord finally settled for twenty. Only a small leaven is needed, only a little center of health can become the means of convalescence for a whole community. That fact measures the awful responsibility of the people of God in the world's cities of destruction.

But there is a climax in this story which is frequently disregarded. It is a terrible climax which has relevance for our own day. However small the saving remnant which God requires for the reconstruction of our communities, it was not forthcoming in Sodom and Gomorrah. Perhaps it is valid to express the surmise that the leavening minority in Sodom may have been quantitatively adequate but that its righteousness was irrelevant for saving Sodom and Gomorrah. One has the uneasy feeling that we are in that position. There is so little health in the whole of our modern civilization that one cannot find the island of order from which to proceed against disorder. Our choices have become terribly circumscribed. Must we finally choose between atomic annihilation or subjection to universal tyranny? If such a day should come we will remember that the mystery of God's sovereignty and mercy transcends the fate of empires and civilizations. He will be exalted though they perish. However, He does not desire their perdition but rather that they turn from their evil ways and live. From us He demands that we work while it is day, since the night cometh when no man can work.

9. *Augustine's Political Realism*

THE TERMS "IDEALISM" and "realism" are not analogous in political and in metaphysical theory; and they are certainly not as precise in political, as in metaphysical, theory. In political and moral theory "realism" denotes the disposition to take all factors in a social and political situation, which offer resistance to established norms, into account, particularly the factors of self-interest and power. In the words of a notorious "realist," Machiavelli, the purpose of the realist is "to follow the truth of the matter rather than the imagination of it; for many have pictures of republics and principalities which have never been seen." This definition of realism implies that idealists are subject to illusions about social realities, which indeed they are. "Idealism" is, in the esteem of its proponents,

119

characterized by loyalty to moral norms and ideals, rather than to self-interest, whether individual or collective. It is, in the opinion of its critics, characterized by a disposition to ignore or be indifferent to the forces in human life which offer resistance to universally valid ideals and norms. This disposition, to which Machiavelli refers, is general whenever men are inclined to take the moral pretensions of themselves or their fellowmen at face value; for the disposition to hide self-interest behind the facade of pretended devotion to values, transcending self-interest, is well-nigh universal. It is, moreover, an interesting human characteristic, proving that the concept of "total depravity," as it is advanced by some Christian realists, is erroneous. Man is a curious creature with so strong a sense of obligation to his fellows that he cannot pursue his own interests without pretending to serve his fellowmen. The definitions of "realists" and "idealists" emphasize disposition, rather than doctrines; and they are therefore bound to be inexact. It must remain a matter of opinion whether or not a man takes adequate account of all the various factors and forces in a social situation. Was Plato a realist, for instance, because he tried to guard against the self-interest of the "guardians" of his ideal state by divesting them of property and reducing their family responsibilities to a minimum? Does this bit of "realism" cancel out the essential unrealism, inherent in ascribing to the "lusts of the body" the force of recalcitrance against the moral norm; or in attributing pure virtue to pure mind?

Augustine was, by general consent, the first great

"realist" in western history. He deserves this distinction
because his picture of social reality in his *civitas dei* gives
an adequate account of the social factions, tensions, and
competitions which we know to be well-nigh universal on
every level of community; while the classical age conceived the order and justice of its *polis* to be a comparatively simple achievement, which would be accomplished
when reason had brought all subrational forces under its
dominion.

This difference in the viewpoint of Augustine and the
classical philosophers lies in Augustine's biblical, rather
than rationalistic, conception of human selfhood with the
ancillary conception of the seat of evil being in the self.
Augustine broke with classical rationalism in his conception of the human self, according to which the self is composed of mind and body, the mind being the seat of virtue because it has the capacity to bring all impulses into
order; and the body, from which come the "lusts and ambitions," being the cause of evil. According to Augustine
the self is an integral unity of mind and body. It is something more than mind and is able to use mind for its purposes. The self has, in fact, a mysterious identity and integrity transcending its functions of mind, memory, and
will. "These three things, memory, understanding, and
love are mine and not their own," he declares, "for they
do what they do not for themselves but for me; or rather
I do it by them. For it is I who remember by memory and
understand by understanding and love by love."[1] It must

[1] *De Trin.*, 15.22.

be observed that the transcendent freedom of this self, including its capacity to defy any rational or natural system into which someone may seek to coordinate it (its capacity for evil) makes it difficult for any philosophy, whether ancient or modern, to comprehend its true dimension. That is why the classical wise men obscured it by fitting its mind into a system of universal mind and the body into the system of nature; and that is also why the modern wise men, for all their rhetoric about the "dignity" of the individual, try to cut down the dimension of human selfhood so that it will seem to fit into a system of nature. This conception of selfhood is drawn from the Bible, rather than from philosophy, because the transcendent self which is present in, though it transcends, all of the functions and effects, is comprehensible only in the dramatic-historical mode of apprehension which characterizes biblical faith. Augustine draws on the insights of neo-Platonism to illustrate the self's power of self-transcendence; but he rejects Plotinus' mystic doctrine, in which the particular self, both human and divine, is lost in a vast realm of undifferentiated being.

Augustine's conception of the evil which threatens the human community on every level is a corollary of his doctrine of selfhood. "Self-love" is the source of evil rather than some residual natural impulse which mind has not yet completely mastered. This excessive love of self, sometimes also defined as pride or *superbia,* is explained as the consequence of the self's abandonment of God as its true end and of making itself "a kind of end." It is this power-

ful self-love or, in a modern term, "egocentricity," this tendency of the self to make itself its own end or even to
make itself the false center of whatever community it in-
habits, which sows confusion into every human community. The power of self-love is more spiritual than the
"lusts of the body," of which Plato speaks; and it corrupts
the processes of the mind more than Plato or Aristotle
knew. That is why Augustine could refute the classical
theory with the affirmation that "it is not the bad body
which causes the good soul to sin but the bad soul which
causes the good body to sin." At other times Augustine
defines the evil in man as the "evil will"; but with the
understanding that it is the self which is evil in the mani-
festation of its will. "For he who extols the whole nature
of the soul as the chief good and condemns the nature of
the flesh as if it were evil, assuredly is fleshly both in the
love of the soul and in the hatred of the flesh."[2] This con-
cise statement of the Christian position surely refutes the
absurd charge of moderns that the Christian faith is "dual-
istic" and generates contempt for the body. It also established the only real basis for a realistic estimate of the
forces of recalcitrance which we must face on all levels
of the human community, particularly for a realistic estimate of the spiritual dimension of these forces and of
the comparative impotence of "pure reason" against them.
Compared with a Christian realism, which is based on
Augustine's interpretation of biblical faith, a great many
modern social and psychological theories, which fancy

[2]*De Civ. Dei*, 15.5.

themselves anti-Platonic or even anti-Aristotelian and
which make much of their pretended "realism," are in
fact no more realistic than the classical philosophers. Thus
modern social and psychological scientists are forever
seeking to isolate some natural impulse such as "aggressiveness" and to manage it; with equal vanity they are
trying to find a surrogate for Plato's and Aristotle's disinterested "reason" in a so-called "scientific method." Their
inability to discover the corruption of self-interest in reason or in man's rational pursuits; and to measure the
spiritual dimension of man's inhumanity and cruelty, gives
an air of sentimentality to the learning of our whole liberal
culture. Thus we have no guidance amid the intricacies
of modern power politics except as the older disciplines,
less enamored of the "methods of natural science," and
the common sense of the man in the street supplies the
necessary insights.

II

Augustine's description of the social effects of human
egocentricity or self-love is contained in his definition of
the life of the "city of this world," the *civitas terrena,*
which he sees as commingled with the *civitas dei.* The
"city of this world" is dominated by self-love to the point
of contempt of God; and is distinguished from the *civitas
dei* which is actuated by the "love of God" to the point
of contempt of self. This "city" is not some little city-state,
as it is conceived in classical thought. It is the whole hu-

man community on its three levels of the family, the commonwealth, and the world. A potential world community is therefore envisaged in Augustine's thought. But, unlike the stoic and modern "idealists," he does not believe that a common humanity or a common reason gives promise of an easy actualization of community on the global level. The world community, declares Augustine "is fuller of dangers as the greater sea is more dangerous."[3] Augustine is a consistent realist in calling attention to the fact that the potential world community may have a common human reason but it speaks in different languages and "Two men, each ignorant of each other's language" will find that "dumb animals, though of a different species, could more easily hold intercourse than they, human beings though they be."[4] This realistic reminder that common linguistic and ethnic cultural forces, which bind the community together on one level, are divisive on the ultimate level, is a lesson which our modern proponents of world government have not yet learned.

Augustine's description of the *civitas terrena* includes an emphasis on the tensions, frictions, competitions of interest, and overt conflicts to which every human community is exposed. Even in the family one cannot rely on friendship "seeing that secret treachery has often broken it up."[5] This bit of realism will seem excessive until we remember that our own generation has as much difficulty

[3]*Ibid.*, 19.7.
[4]*Ibid.*, 19.7.
[5]*Ibid.*, 19.5.

in preserving the peace and integrity in the smallest and most primordial community, the family, as in integrating community on the highest global level.

The *civitas terrena* is described as constantly subject to an uneasy armistice between contending forces, with the danger that factional disputes may result in "bloody insurrection" at any time. Augustine's realism prompts him to challenge Cicero's conception of a commonwealth as rooted in a "compact of justice." Not so, declares Augustine. Commonwealths are bound together by a common love, or collective interest, rather than by a sense of justice; and they could not maintain themselves without the imposition of power. "Without injustice the republic would neither increase nor subsist. The imperial city to which the republic belongs could not rule over provinces without recourse to injustice. For it is unjust for some men to rule over others."[6]

This realism has the merit of describing the power realities which underlie all large scale social integrations whether in Egypt or Babylon or Rome, where a dominant city-state furnished the organizing power for the Empire. It also describes the power realities of national states, even democratic ones, in which a group, holding the dominant form of social power, achieves oligarchic rule, no matter how much modern democracy may bring such power under social control. This realism in regard to the facts which underlie the organizing or governing power refutes the charge of modern liberals that a realistic analysis of

[6]*Ibid.,* 19.21.

social forces makes for state absolutism; so that a mild illusion in regard to human virtue is necessary to validate democracy. Realistic pessimism did indeed prompt both Hobbes and Luther to an unqualified endorsement of state power; but that is only because they were not realistic enough. They saw the dangers of anarchy in the egotism of the citizens but failed to perceive the dangers of tyranny in the selfishness of the ruler. Therefore they obscured the consequent necessity of placing checks upon the ruler's self-will. Augustine's realism was indeed excessive. On the basis of his principles he could not distinguish between government and slavery, both of which were supposedly the rule over man by man and were both a consequence of, and remedy for, sin; nor could he distinguish between a commonwealth and a robber band, for both were bound together by collective interest; "For even thieves must hold together or they cannot effect what they intend." The realism fails to do justice to the sense of justice in the constitution of the Roman Empire; or for that matter to the sense of justice in a robber band. For even thieves will fall out if they cannot trust each other to divide the loot, which is their common aim, equitably. But the excessive emphasis upon the factors of power and interest, a wholesome corrective to Cicero's and modern Ciceronian moralistic illusions, is not fatal to the establishment of justice so long as the dangers of tyranny are weighed as realistically as the dangers of anarchy.

Augustine's realistic attitude toward government rests partly upon the shrewd observation that social peace and

order are established by a dominant group within some
level of community; and that this group is not exempt
from the corruption of self-interest merely because the
peace of society has been entrusted to it. (One thinks incidentally how accurately the Augustinian analysis fits
both the creative and the ambiguous character of the
American hegemony in the social cohesion of the free
world.) The realism is partly determined by his conception of a "natural order" which he inherited from the early
Christian fathers, who in turn took it from that part of
the Stoic theory which emphasized the primordial or
primitive as the natural. This Stoic and Christian primitivism has the merit of escaping the errors of those natural
law theories which claim to find a normative moral order
amid the wide variety of historic forms or even among
the most universal of these forms. The freedom of man
makes these Stoic conceptions of the "natural" impossible.
But it has the weakness which characterizes all primitivism, whether Stoic, Christian, or Romantic, for it
makes primitive social forms normative. A primitive norm,
whether of communal property relations or unorganized
social cohesion, may serve provisionally as an occasion
for the criticism of the institutions of an advancing civilization, more particularly the institutions of property and
government; but it has the disadvantage of prompting indiscriminate criticism. This lack of discrimination is obvious in primitivistic Stoicism, in early Christianity, in
seventeenth-century Cromwellian sectarianism, in Roman-
ticism, and in Marxism and anarchism.

Augustine expressed this idea of a primitive social norm as follows: "This is the prescribed order of nature. It is thus that God created man. For 'let them,' He says, 'have dominion over the fish of the sea and the fowl of the air and over every creeping thing, which creepeth on the earth.' He did not intend that His rational creature, made in His image, should have dominion over anything but irrational creation—not man over man but man over beasts. And hence the righteous men of primitive times were made shepherds of cattle rather than kings of men."[7] This primitivism avoids the later error of the absolute sanctification of government. But its indiscriminate character is apparent by his failure to recognize the difference between legitimate and illegitimate, between ordinate and inordinate subordination of man to man. Without some form of such subordination the institutions of civilization could not exist.

III

If Augustine's realism is contained in his analysis of the *civitas terrena*, his refutation of the idea that realism must lead to cynicism or relativism is contained in his definition of the *civitas dei*, which he declares to be "commingled" with the "city of this word" and which has the "love of God" rather than the "love of self" as its guiding principle. The tension between the two cities is occasioned by the fact that, while egotism is "natural" in the

[7] *Ibid.*, 19.15.

sense that it is universal, it is not natural in the sense that it does not conform to man's nature who transcends himself indeterminately and can only have God rather than self for his end. A realism becomes morally cynical or nihilistic when it assumes that the universal characteristic in human behavior must also be regarded as normative. The biblical account of human behavior, upon which Augustine bases his thought, can escape both illusion and cynicism because it recognizes that the corruption of human freedom may make a behavior pattern universal without making it normative. Good and evil are not determined by some fixed structure of human existence. Man, according to the biblical view, may use his freedom to make himself falsely the center of existence; but this does not change the fact that love rather than self-love is the law of his existence in the sense that man can only be healthy and his communities at peace if man is drawn out of himself and saved from the self-defeating consequences of self-love. There are several grave errors in Augustine's account of love and of the relation of love to self-love; but before considering them we might well first pay tribute to his approach to political problems. The virtue of making love, rather than justice, into the norm for the community may seem, at first blush, to be dubious. The idea of justice seems much more relevant than the idea of love, particularly for the collective relationships of men. The medieval tradition which makes the justice of a rational "natural law" normative even for Christians when they consider the necessities of a sinful world, seems much

more realistic than modern forms of sentimental Protestantism which regards love as a simple alternative to self-
love, which could be achieved if only we could preach
the idea persuasively enough to beguile men from the one
to the other. Augustine's doctrine of love as the final norm
must be distinguished from modern sentimental versions
of Christianity which regard love as a simple possibility
and which think it significant to assert the obvious propo-
sition that all conflicts in the community would be avoided
if only people and nations would love one another. Augustine's approach differs from modern forms of sentimental
perfectionism in the fact that he takes account of the
power and persistence of egotism, both individual and
collective, and seeks to establish the most tolerable form
of peace and justice under conditions set by human sin.
He inherited the tradition of monastic perfection; and he
allows it as a vent for the Christian impulse toward individual perfection, without however changing the emphasis upon the duty of the Christian to perfect the peace of
the city of this world. Furthermore, he raises questions
about monastic perfection which, when driven home by
the Reformation, were to undermine the whole system.
"I venture to say," he writes, "that it is good for those who
observe continence and are proud of it, to fall that they
may be humbled. For what benefit is it to anyone in whom
is the virtue of continence, if pride holds sway? He is but
despising that by which man is born in striving after that
which led to satan's fall . . . holy virginity is better than
conjugal chastity . . . but if we add two other things,

pride and humility . . . which is better, pride or humility?
. . . I have no doubt that a humble married woman is to
be preferred to a proud virgin . . . a mother holds a lesser
place in the Kingdom of God because she has been married, than the daughter, seeing that she is a virgin. . . .
But if thy mother has been proud and thou humble, she
will have some sort of place and thou none."[8]

While Augustine's doctrine of love is thus not to be
confused with modern sentimentalities which do not take
the power of self-love seriously, one may well wonder
whether an approach to politics which does not avail itself of the calculations of justice, may be deemed realistic.
We have already noted that Augustine avails himself of the
theory of the "natural law," only in the primordial version
of the theory. If primordial conditions of a "natural order"
are not to be defined as normative, the only alternative is to
assume a "rational order" to which the whole of historical
life conforms. Aquinas, in fact, constructed his theory of the
natural law upon classical, and primarily Aristotelian, foundations. It was the weakness of both classical and medieval
theories that they assumed an order in history, conform-
ing to the uniformities of nature. Aristotle was aware of
deviations in history, greater than those in nature; but he
believed that there was nevertheless one form "which was
marked by nature as the best." There is, in other words,
no place in this theory of natural law for the endlessly
unique social configurations which human beings, in their
freedom over natural necessity, construct. The proponents

[8]Sermon cccIIV, ix, 9.

of "natural law" therefore invariably introduce some historically contingent norm or social structure into what
they regard as God's inflexible norm. That was the weakness of both classical and medieval social theory; and for
that matter of the natural law theories of the bourgeois
Parties of the eighteenth century, who had found that
they regarded as a more empirically perceived "natural
law"; but the modern empirical intelligence was no more
capable than the deductive rational processes of classical
and medieval times to construct a social norm, not colored
by the interests of the constructor, thus introducing the
taint of ideology into the supposed sanctities of law. We
must conclude therefore that Augustine was wise in avoiding the alleged solution of a natural law theory, which was
the basis of so much lack of realism in both the classical
and the medieval period, and which can persist today
long after the Aristotelian idea of fixed form for historical
events has been overcome, as the dogma of a religious
system which makes its supposed sanctities into an article
of faith. His conception of the radical freedom of man,
derived from the biblical view, made it impossible to accept the idea of fixed forms of human behavior and of
social organization, analogous to those of nature, even as
he opposed the classical theory of historical cycles. Furthermore, his conception of human selfhood and of the
transcendence of the self over its mind, made it impossible
to assume the identity of the individual reason with a universal reason, which lies at the foundation of the classical
and medieval natural law theories. It is in fact something

of a mystery how the Christian insights into human nature and history, expressed by Augustine, could have been subordinated to classical thought with so little sense of the conflict between them in the formulations of Thomas Aquinas; and how they should have become so authoritative in Roman Catholicism without more debate between Augustinian and Thomistic emphases.

Augustine's formula for leavening the city of this world with the love of the city of God is more adequate than classical and medieval thought, both in doing justice to the endless varieties of historical occasions and configurations and in drawing upon the resources of love rather than law in modifying human behavior.

Every "earthly peace," declares Augustine, is good as far as it goes. "But they will not have it long for they used it not well while they had it." That is, unless some larger love or loyalty qualifies the self-interest of the various groups, this collective self-interest will expose the community to either an overt conflict of competing groups or to the injustice of a dominant group which "when it is victorious it will become vice's slave." Let us use some examples from current national and international problems to illustrate the Augustinian thesis. There is, or was, a marked social tension between the middle classes of industrial owners and the industrial workers in all modern industrial nations. In some of them, for instance in Germany and France, this tension led to overt forms of the class conflict. In others such as Britain, the smaller European nations and America, this tension was progressively resolved by various accommodations of interest. Wherein lay the difference? It did not lie in the possession of more adequate formulae of justice in some nations than in others. The difference lay in the fact that in some nations the various interest groups had, in addition to their collective interest, a "sense of justice," a disposition to "give each man his due" and a loyalty to the national community which qualified the interest struggle. Now, that spirit of justice is identical with the spirit of love, except at the highest level of the spirit of love, where it becomes purely sacrificial and engages in no calculation of what the due of each man may be. Two forms of love, the love of the other and the love of the community, were potent in short in modifying the acerbities and injustices of the class struggle. The two forms of love availed themselves of various calculations of justice in arriving at and defining their *ad hoc* agreements. But the factors in each nation and in each particular issue were too variable to allow for the application of any general rules or formulae of justice. Agreements were easier in fact if too much was not claimed for these formulae. Certain "principles" of justice, as distinguished from formulas or prescriptions, were indeed operative, such as liberty, equality, and loyalty to covenants; but these principles will be recognized as no more than the law of love in its various facets.

In the same manner the international community is exposed to exactly the tensions and competitions of interest which Augustine describes. There are no formulas of justice or laws which will prevent these tensions from reaching overt conflict, if the collective interest of each nation is not modified by its loyalty to a higher value such as the common civilization of the free nations. Where this common loyalty is lacking, as in our relation with Russia, no formula can save us from the uneasy peace in which we live. The character of this peace is just as tentative as Augustine described it. Whenever common loves or loyalties, or even common fears, lay the foundation for community, it must of course be our business to perfect it by calculations of justice which define our mutual responsibilities as exactly as possible.

It must be noted that the Augustinian formula for the leavening influence of a higher upon a lower loyalty or love, is effective in preventing the lower loyalty from involving itself in self-defeat. It corrects the "realism" of those who are myopically realistic by seeing only their own interests and failing thereby to do justice to their interests where they are involved with the interests of others. There are modern realists, for instance, who, in their reaction to abstract and vague forms of international idealism, counsel the nation to consult only its own interests. In a sense collective self-interest is so consistent that it is superfluous to advise it. But a consistent self-interest on the part of a nation will work against its interests because it will fail to do justice to the broader and longer interests, which are involved with the interests of other nations. A narrow national loyalty on our part, for instance, will obscure our long range interests where they are involved with those of a whole alliance of free nations.

Thus the loyalty of a leavening portion of a nation's citizens to a value transcending national interest will save a "realistic" nation from defining its interests in such narrow and short range terms as to defeat the real interests of the nation.

IV

We have acknowledged some weaknesses in the Augustinian approach to the political order which we must now define and examine more carefully. Non-Catholics commonly criticize Augustine's alleged identification of the *civitas dei* with the visible Church. But we must absolve him of this charge or insist on a qualification of the criticism. He does indeed accept the Catholic doctrine, which had grown up before his day; and he defines the visible Church as the only perfect society. There are passages in which he seems to assume that it is possible to claim for the members of the Church that they are solely actuated by the *amor dei*. But he introduces so many reservations to this assertion that he may well be defined in this, as in other instances, as the father of both Catholicism and the Reformation. Of the Church, Augustine declared, "by faith she is a virgin. In the flesh she has few holy virgins"[9] or again: "God will judge the wicked and the good. The evil cannot now be separated from the good but must be suffered for a season. The wicked may be with us on the threshing floor . . . in the

[9]Sermon CCXIII, vii, 7.

barn they cannot be."[10] The reservations which he made
upon the identification of the Church and the kingdom
laid the foundations for the later Reformation position.
But these reservations about the sinners who might be
present in the visible Church cannot obscure a graver
error in his thought. This error is probably related to his
conception of grace which does not allow for the phenomenon, emphasized by the Reformation, that men may
be redeemed in the sense that they consciously turn from
self to Christ as their end, and yet they are not redeemed
from the corruption of egotism which expresses itself, even
in the lives of the saints. This insight is most succinctly
expressed in Luther's phrase *"justus et peccator simul"*
(righteous and sinners at once). When Augustine distinguished between the "two loves" which characterize
the "two cities," the love of God and the love of self, and
when he pictured the world as a commingling of the two
cities, he does not recognize that the commingling is due,
not to the fact that two types of people dwell together
but because the conflict between love and self-love is in
every soul. It is particularly important to recognize this
fact in political analyses; for nothing is more obvious than
that personal dedication is no guarantee against the involvement of the dedicated individual in some form of
collective egotism.

We have frequently referred to Augustine's definition
of the "two loves" which inform the "two cities" of which
"the one is selfish and the other social," the one loving

10*Comm. on Ps.* CXI, 9.

self to the point of the contempt of God and the other
loving God to the point of contempt of self. The question
is whether Bishop Nygren[11] is right in defining the Augustinian conception of *amor dei* as rooted in a classical rather
than a biblical concept.

In defense of Augustine it must be said that he is not
insensible to the two facets of the love commandment
and therefore does not define the *amor dei* in purely mystical terms as a flight from this world. He insists on the
contrary that the *amor dei* is "social" and he offers the
concord among brethren as a proof of the love of God.
But nevertheless Nygren is right in suggesting that the
thought of Plotinus has colored Augustine's conceptions
sufficiently so that the *agape* of the New Testament is
misinterpreted by Augustine's conception of *charitas* and
amor dei. The *agape* form of love in the New Testament
fails to be appreciated particularly in two of its facets:
A) the equality of the "two loves," the love of the neighbor and the love of God (enforced in the Scripture by the
words "the Second is like unto it") is violated by Augustine under the influence of Plotinus even as a later medieval Catholic mystic, St. John of the Cross, violates it
when he regarded the love of the creature as a ladder
which might lead us to the love of God, but must be subordinated to the latter. Augustine wants us to love the
neighbor for the sake of God, which may be a correct
formulation; but he wants us to prove the genuineness of
our love of God in the love of the neighbor, or by leading

[11]Anders Nygren, in *Agape and Eros*.

him to God. Thus the meeting of the neighbor's need
without regard to any ultimate religious intention is emptied of meaning. The love of the neighbor is for him not
part of a double love commandment but merely the instrument of a single love commandment which bids us
flee all mortality including the neighbor in favor of the
immutable good. B) The second facet of the *agape* concept of the New Testament which tends to be obscured
is the notion of sacrificial love, the absurd principle of the
Cross, the insistence that the self must sacrifice itself for
the other. It is not fair to Augustine to say that he neglects
this facet of meaning for he seems to emphasize it so constantly. He comes closest to its meaning when he deals
with the relation of humility to love. Yet it seems fair to
say that he was sufficiently imbued by classical mystical
thought forms so that the emphasis lies always upon the
worthiness or unworthiness of the object of our love; the
insistence is that only God and not some mutable "good"
or person is worthy of our love. This is a safeguard against
all forms of idolatry. But it does not answer another important question: when I love a person or a community
do I love myself in them or do I truly love them? Is my
love a form of alteregoism? The Augustinian *amor dei*
assumes that the self in its smallness cannot contain itself
within itself and therefore it is challenged to go out from
itself to the most ultimate end. But it hardly reveals the
full paradox of self-realization through self-giving which
a scandal in the field of rational ethics as the Cross is a
scandal in the field of rational religion. Yet it is the source

of ultimate wisdom. For the kind of self-giving which has
self-realization as its result must not have self-realization
as its conscious end; otherwise the self by calculating its
enlargement will not escape from itself completely enough
to be enlarged. The weakness of Augustine in obscuring
these facets of the *agape* principle may be illustrated,
without unfairness I hope, by referring to his treatment
of family love. He questions the love of mate or children
as the final form of love, but not for New Testament reasons. He does not say: "When you love your wife and
children are you maybe really loving yourself in them and
using them as the instruments of your self-aggrandise-
ments?" He declares instead, in effect, you must not love
your family too unreservedly because your wife and children are mortal. They also belong to the "rivers of Babylon," and, if you give them absolute devotion, the hour
of bereavement will leave you desolate. Of course Augustine is too much the Christian to engage in a consistent
mystic depreciation of the responsibilities and joys of this
earthly life. After all, his whole strategy for the "commingling" of the two cities revolves around the acceptance
of the ordinary responsibilities of home and state but in
performing these tasks for the ultimate, rather than the
immediate end. "What then?" he asks. "Shall all perish
who marry and are given in marriage, who till the fields
and build houses? No, but those who put their trust in
these things, who prefer them to God, who for the sake
of these things are quick to offend God, these will perish.
But those who either do not use these things or who use

them as though they used them not, trusting more in Him
who gave them than in the things given, understanding
in them His consolation and mercy, and who are not absorbed in these gifts lest they fall away from the giver.
These are they whom the day will not overtake as a thief
unprepared."[12] We must not, in criticizing Augustine for
neo-Platonic elements in his thought, obscure the Christian elements which will be equally an offense to modern
men who regard the world as self-sufficing and self-ex-
planatory, who reject as absurd the Christian faith that
there is not only a mystery behind and above the world
of observed phenomena and intelligible meanings, but
that it is a mystery whose meaning has been disclosed as
a love which elicits our answering love. This modern generation with its confidence in a world without mystery,
and without meaning beyond simple intelligibility, will
not be beguiled from its unbelief by a reminder that its
emancipation from God has betrayed it into precisely
those idolatries, the worship of false gods, the dedication
to finite values as if they were ultimate, of which Augustine spoke. But it must be recorded nevertheless as a significant fact of modern history. While it is an offence to
regard communism as the inevitable end-product of secularism, as some Christians would have us believe, it is
only fair to point out that the vast evils of modern communism come ironically to a generation which thought it
would be easy to invest all the spiritual capital of men,
who mysteriously transcend the historical process, in some

[12]*Comm. on Ps.* cxx, 3.

value or end within that process; and communism is merely the most pathetic and cruel of the idolatrous illusions of this generation.

We must be clear about the fact that all the illusions about man's character and history which made it so difficult for either the classical or the modern age to come to terms with the vexing problems of our togetherness, seem to stem from efforts to understand man in both his grandeur and his misery by "integrating" him into some natural or rational system of coherence. Thereby they denied the mystery of his transcendence over every process which points to another mystery beyond himself without which man is not only a mystery to himself but a misunderstood being.

We cannot deny that from a Christian standpoint the world is like a "river of Babylon" to use Augustine's symbol; and that Augustine is right in suggesting that ultimately we cannot find peace if we are merely tossed down the river of time. We must find security in that which is not carried down the river. "Observe however," declares Augustine in a simile which will seem strange to generations which have made the "rivers of Babylon," the stream of temporal events, into forces of redemption; but which will not seem so strange as the modern experience proves history as such to be less redemptive than we had believed. "The rivers of Babylon are all things which are here loved, and pass away. For example, one man loves to practice husbandry, to grow rich by it, to employ his mind on it, to get his pleasure from it. Let

him observe the issue and see that what he has loved is
not a foundation of Jerusalem, but a river of Babylon.
Another says, it is a grand thing to be a soldier; all farmers
fear those who are soldiers, are subservient to them, trem-
ble at them. If I am a farmer, I shall fear soldiers; if a
soldier, farmers will fear me. Madman! thou hast cast thy-
self headlong into another river of Babylon, and that still
more turbulent and sweeping. Thou wishest to be feared
by thy inferior; fear Him Who is greater than thou. He
who fears thee may on a sudden become greater than
thou, but He Whom thou oughtest to fear will never become less. To be an advocate, says another, is a grand
thing; eloquence is most powerful; always to have clients
hanging on the lips of their eloquent advocate, and from
his words looking for loss or gain, death or life, ruin or
security. Thou knowest not whither thou hast cast thy-
self. This too is another river of Babylon, and its roaring
sound is the din of the waters dashing against the rocks.
Mark that it flows, that it glides on; beware, for it carries
things away with it. To sail the seas, says another, and
to trade is a grand thing—to know many lands, to make
gains from every quarter, never to be answerable to any
powerful man in thy country, to be always travelling, and
to feed thy mind with the diversity of the nations and the
business met with, and to return enriched by the increase
of thy gains. This too is a river of Babylon. When will the
gains stop? When wilt thou have confidence and be secure
in the gains thou makest? The richer thou art, the more
fearful wilt thou be. Once shipwrecked, thou wilt come

forth stripped of all, and rightly wilt bewail thy fate *in* the rivers of Babylon, because thou wouldest not sit down and weep *upon* the rivers of Babylon.

"But there are other citizens of the holy Jerusalem, understanding their captivity, who mark how human wishes and the diverse lusts of men, hurry and drag them hither and thither, and drive them into the sea. They see this, and do not throw themselves into the rivers of Babylon, but sit down upon the rivers of Babylon and upon the rivers of Babylon weep, either for those who are being carried away by them, or for themselves whose deserts have placed them in Babylon."[13]

Whatever the defects of the Augustine approach may be, we must acknowledge his immense superiority both over those who preceded him and who came after him. A part of that superiority was due to his reliance upon biblical rather than idealistic or naturalistic conceptions of selfhood. But that could not have been the only cause, else Christian systems before and after him would not have been so inferior. Or were they inferior either because they subordinated the biblical-dramatic conception of human selfhood too much to the rationalistic scheme, as was the case with medieval Christianity culminating in the thought of Thomas Aquinas? or because they did not understand that the corruption of human freedom could not destroy the original dignity of man, as was the case with the Reformation with its doctrines of sin, bordering on total depravity and resulting in Luther's too pessimistic

[13]*Comm. on Ps.* CXXXVI, 3, 4.

approach to political problems? As for secular thought, it has difficulty in approaching Augustine's realism without falling into cynicism or in avoiding nihilism without falling into sentimentality. Hobbes' realism was based on an insight which he shared with Augustine, namely, that in all historical encounters the mind is the servant and not the master of the self. But he failed to recognize that the self which thus made the mind its instrument was a corrupted and not a "normal" self. Modern "realists" know the power of collective self-interest as Augustine did; but they do not understand its blindness. Modern pragmatists understood the irrelevance of fixed and detailed norms; but they do not understand that love must take the place as the final norm for these inadequate norms. Modern liberal Christians know that love is the final norm for man; but they fall into sentimentality because they fail to measure the power and persistence of self-love. Thus Augustine, whatever may be the defects of his approach to political reality, and whatever may be the dangers of a too slavish devotion to his insights, nevertheless proves himself a more reliable guide than any known thinker. A generation which finds its communities imperiled and in decay from the smallest and most primordial community, the family, to the largest and most recent, the potential world community, might well take counsel of Augustine in solving its perplexities.

10. *Love and Law in Protestantism and Catholicism*

THE WHOLE QUESTION about the relation of love to law in Christian thought is really contained in the question how love is the fulfillment of the law. The analysis of this issue may well begin with a definition of the nature of law. Subjectively considered, law is distinguished by some form of restraint or coercion, or, as Aquinas puts it, it is the direction to "perform virtuous acts by reason of some outward cause." The compulsion may be the force and prestige of the mores and customs of a community, persuading or compelling an individual to act contrary to his inclinations. But there is also an inner compulsion of law. It is the compulsion of conscience, the force of the sense of obligation, operating against other impulses

in the personality. If there is no friction or tension between duty and inclination law is, at least in one sense,
dissolved into love.

Materially, law usually represents detailed prescriptions of duties and obligations which the self owes to itself, to God, and to its neighbors. There may of course
be general principles of law which gather together the
logic of detailed prescriptions, as for instance the proposi-
tion, defined in Catholic thought as the "preamble" of the
natural law, "that we ought to do good and avoid evil";
or Jesus' own summary of the law and the prophets. But
that summary is, significantly, the "law of love" and therefore no longer purely law, but a law transcending law.
Some degree of detail is characteristic of pure law. The
"positive law" of historic communities gains its force
primarily from its specificity. Many a law has been annulled by our Supreme Court on the ground that "vague-
ness" invalidated it. Even if we do not accept the Catholic
theory of a highly specific "natural law" we all do accept
principles of justice which transcend the positive enact-
ments of historic states and which are less specific and
not so sharply defined as positive law, and yet more specific than the law of love. These are generated in the customs and mores of communities; and they may rise to
universal norms which seem to have their source not in
particular communities but in the common experience of
mankind.

The question of how love is related to law must be
considered in terms of both the subjective and the ma-

terial dimensions of both love and law. Subjectively, the question is how the experience of love, in which the "ought" is transcended, nevertheless contains a "thou shalt." Materially, the question is how the indeterminate possibilities of love are related to the determinate and specified obligations defined by law. The dialectical relation of love to law as both its fulfillment and its end (*pleroma* and *telos*), as fulfilling all possibilities of law and yet as standing in contradiction to it ("The law was given by Moses, but grace and truth came by Jesus Christ," John 1:17), is the basis and the problem of all Catholic and Protestant speculations on the relation of love to law.

In this debate Catholic thought, both in its classical version and in such a modern treatise as D'Arcy's *Mind and Heart of Love,* is more inclined than the Reformation to interpret love as *pleroma* of everything intended in nature and in law. But it is also inclined to interpret love as yet a more rigorous law, thus obscuring the elements of ecstasy and spontaneity, which are the marks of "grace." Reformation thought (or at least Lutheran thought, for Calvin does not deviate essentially from the Catholic version), on the other hand, is much nearer in its apprehension of a dimension of love which transcends law and even contradicts it; but it usually fails to do justice to love as the fulfillment of law and therefore tends to obscure the intimate relation between love and justice. Modern liberal Protestantism is inclined to equate law and love by its effort to comprehend all law within the love commandment. It does not deny the higher dimensions of love which express themselves in sacrifice, forgiveness, individual sympathy, and universal love, but it regards them as simple possibilities and thereby obscures the tensions between love and law, both on the subjective and the objective side.

II

In terms of the subjective dimension of the problem of love and law is the problem of the "push" of duty and the "pull" of grace. If the law of love comes to us as a "thou shalt" it is obviously a law. We can have a sense of obligation toward the interests of others without a definition of specific obligations. In this case love is simply the summary of all our obligations. This is why Thomas Aquinas includes love in the "old law" though this inclusion is inconsistent with his definition of the "old law" as the "law of fear" and his confining it to the restraint of actions rather than attitudes, to "restraining the hand rather than the will." On the other hand, love means a perfect accord between duty and inclination in such a way that duty is not felt as duty and "we love the things that thou commandest." This second aspect of love is disregarded in Kant's interpretation of love, for instance. For him the sense of obligation in its most universal and least specific form is identical with the law of love.

In Luther's exposition of the life of grace, "law" and "conscience" are left behind with sin and self. This freedom from the sense of "ought" is described by him as an ecstatic experience in which the self calculates no advantages, rises above every form of prudence, and feels itself at one with Christ, being motivated purely by a sense of gratitude for the divine forgiveness. Brunner stands in the Lutheran tradition when he also emphasizes this transcendence over the "ought" and declares that "if we feel we ought it is a proof that we cannot." It is a question whether this point of "grace" is understood by Calvin at all. For his ethic is one of obedience to the divine law. Love is a summary of this law, but he is also careful to spell it out in specific detail. The detail is as specific as Catholic "natural law" except that he draws the details not from the intuitions of reason but from "various portions of Scripture." He is convinced that we need this law in specific form to guide our conscience, corrupted by sin; and there is no suggestion that law and conscience do not operate in the state of grace.

This contrast between the conception of an identity of love and the sense of obligation, on the one hand, and a contradiction between them, on the other, is the proof of a complicated relationship between love and law in both the subjective and the objective sphere. What is described by Luther as freedom from law may well conform to momentary heights of spiritual experience in which there is such a "pull" of grace (which may include everything from ecstatic religious experience to the "common grace" of family love) that we are not conscious of any "ought" or any sense of obligation. But it may be questioned whether it can describe anything more than such

moments. It certainly does not describe the ongoing experience of even the most consecrated Christian, particularly not if it is true about him, as Luther asserts, that he
is *"justus et peccator simul."* For if he remains a sinner
it must be true of him that he feels the tension between
his self-interest, his anxieties and insecurities and the obligation to forget himself for the sake of his concern for
others. It may well be that everything defined as the
"sense of justice" is an expression of the law of love within
the limits of law. There are some aspects of the law of
love, objectively considered, which are more clearly in
the realm of duty than in the realm of grace. The injunction "If ye love them that love you what thanks have ye?"
for instance, points to the universalistic tendencies in the
law of love. It expresses our obligations beyond the boun-
daries of the natural communities of family, tribe, and
nation. But paradoxically the love within the family may
be by "grace" rather than law, while the love of "mankind" must be by law. That is, there may be such conjugal
or paternal or filial affection as disposes us to seek the
good of wife, husband, or child without any sense of duty,
"common grace" or "habitual grace" having drawn the
self beyond itself and out of itself into the lives of others.
But our concern for those beyond our circle, our obligation to the peoples of the world and the community of
mankind, comes to us very much with the push of the
"ought" against the force of our more parochial habits of
grace.

Yet on the other hand, pure obligation, while not so

impotent as Brunner suggests, is more impotent than generally recognized, which is why purely moralistic sermons,
which always tell us what we ought to do, tend to be
boring. The best modern psychiatry, when dealing with
the problem of delinquency in children, significantly does
not preach to them what they ought to do, not even that
they "ought to accept themselves." It insists that they
must be accepted, must find security in the love of others,
out of which security they gain sufficient freedom from
self to "let go" and love others. Common grace, in short,
rather than law is offered as a cure for their ills. It might
be added that a good deal of modern Christian teaching
about Christian love may be by comparison very loveless.
For the preacher chides his congregation endlessly for not
meeting the most ultimate possibilities of the law of love,
such as sacrifice, forgiveness, and uncalculated freedom
from self, as if these were simple possibilities of the will.
Thus the law of love becomes the occasion for loveless
castigation because it is not recognized that, on the subjective side, love is a curious compound of willing through
the strength of the sense of obligation and of willing not
by the strength of our will but by the strength which
enters the will through grace. This defect in the liberal
Protestant attitude toward love is the subjective aspect of
its lack of a doctrine of grace. The objective aspect, which
must be considered subsequently, is revealed in its lack
of distinction between love and justice. In both aspects
the basis of the defect lies in the failure to appreciate the
force of self-love in life. The consequence of this failure

creates the belief that love is a law which can be easily fulfilled if only the preacher will establish its validity and present it persuasively. Grace, whether "common" or "saving," has meaning only when life is measured at the limits of human possibilities and it is recognized that there are things we ought to do which we cannot do merely by the strength of our willing but which may become possible because we are assisted by the help which others give us by their love, by the strength which accrues to our will in moments of crisis, and by the saving grace of the Spirit of God indwelling our spirit.

III

Subjectively we have defined the problem of love and law as the problem of the relation of duty to grace. Materially the problem is the relation of love as the sum and total of all law and of love as defining indeterminate possibilities, transcending law. These points of indeterminacy in the law of love correspond to the indeterminate character of human freedom. In so far as man has a determinate structure, it is possible to state the "essential nature" of human existence to which his actions ought to conform and which they should fulfill. But in so far as he has the freedom to transcend structure, standing beyond himself and beyond every particular social situation, every law is subject to indeterminate possibilities which finally exceed the limits of any specific definition of what he "ought" to do. Yet they do not stand completely outside of law, if law is defined in terms of man's essential nature. For this indeterminate freedom is a part of his essential nature.

The points at which the transcendence of love over law are clearest are four, of which one point may really belong to the realm of law: a) The freedom of man over every historic situation means that his obligation to others cannot be limited to partial communities of nature and history, to family, tribe, or nation. ("If ye love them that love you what thanks have ye?") Love acknowledges no natural bounds and is universal in scope. ("Whoso loveth father or mother more than me is not worthy of me.") This first element in the indeterminacy of love has already been described as being, in one respect at least, within the limits of law. For it describes the sum total of all our obligations to our fellow men without specific detail. It is thus the summary of all law. It may come to us subjectively in the force of obligation in opposition to more parochial forms of love which are nourished by common grace.

Yet this universalistic aspect of the law of love is frequently made to bear the whole burden of the idea of love beyond law. In the thought of Augustine, the love of God, as distinguished from the love of any creature, defines the difference between the realm of grace and the real of nature. Augustine makes the mistake of never being concerned whether, in a relation of love, we rise to the point of loving the other person for his own sake or only for our sake. His concern is always whether we love the

person for his own sake or for God's sake. This is to say
he is afraid that love of the other may degenerate into
idolatry. He compounds this error by insisting that the
love of the neighbor must express itself not so much in
meeting his needs as in leading him to God. "So when
one . . . is commanded to love his neighbor as himself,
what else is he enjoined than that he shall commend him
to the love of God?"[1]

In Catholic asceticism the universalism of the Christian love commandment becomes one basis for celibacy
and virginity. (The other basis is its attitude toward sex.)
The institution of the family is destroyed in order that
there may be no parochial impediment to universal love.
This is one aspect of the Catholic strategy of dealing with
the dimension of love which transcends law in its "counsels of perfection." The difference between commandment
and counsel, declares Aquinas, is "that a commandment
implies obligation whereas a counsel is left to the option
of the one to whom it is given."[2] This definition of the
universal aspects of the law of love in its universalistic
indeterminacy, as a more rigorous law, which is too rigorous for the majority of Christians "because their disposition is not inclined" to it but must be kept by the few
who have the "fitness" to observe it, is a part of the whole
Catholic strategy of creating two grades of Christians:
a) those who live by the law of love within the limits of
love as law; and b) those who live by the law of love

[1]*De Civ. Dei* x, 3.
[2]*Summa* III Quest. 108.3.

beyond the limits of natural law. The difficulty with this strategy is that it removes the element of the indeterminate in the law of love as a resource upon all Christian life and it reduces the ultimate possibilities of love to the dimension of a yet more rigorous law.

This defect in Catholic thought arises from the incorporation of Stoic natural law into Christian ethics. For Stoic natural law assumes a determinate human freedom and falsely equates the fixed structures of nature and the less fixed structures of human nature. The supposedly fixed structures of human nature are the basis of a law which states those things to be done and not to be done "which follow in an inevitable manner from the fact that man is man" (Maritain). But the indeterminate character of human freedom and the variety and uniqueness of historic occasions produce fewer things than supposed in Catholic natural law theory, about which one may be sure that they must be done or not done. Everything one does stands under more ultimate possibilities of love, which can not merely be reserved for the celibate who has decided that he will make one extra effort "to be perfect."

In Catholic mysticism (particularly clearly in the mysticism of St. John of the Cross) the love of God is set in complete contradiction to the love of the neighbor in such a way that the love of the creature is merely a step-ladder to the love of God, which must be abandoned when the love of God (universal love) is reached. All of these errors arise from adding the biblical conceptions of freedom, sin, and grace to a classical, rationalistic definition of the structure of human nature. In this rationalism there is an inadequate conception of human selfhood, particularly of its indeterminate possibilities of both love and self-love.

But the same error creeps into some Protestant emphases on the universal aspects of the love commandment. Kierkegaard, despite his existentialist understanding of human selfhood, presents a legalistic version of universal love in his *Works of Love,* according to which the love of a person in his uniqueness and in the uniqueness of a particular relation (as wife or husband, for instance) has nothing to do with "Christian" love. Christian love is a universal love which proves itself by regarding the loved self as anonymously as possible. The force of love is lacking in every element of spontaneity and "grace." It is the force of law and of conscience. Kierkegaard, in short, defines Christian love in precisely those terms with Brunner, with contrasting one-sidedness, regards as outside the dimension of Christian love. For Christian love reveals itself for Brunner only in uniquely personal and intimate relations. Kierkegaard writes:

> Christianity has not come into the world to teach you how specifically to love your wife or your friend but . . . how in common humanity you shall love all men. . . . Love is a matter of conscience and hence not a matter of impulse or inclination.[3]

The universalistic dimension of the love command-

3*Works of Love,* p. 116.

ment is, in short, both within and beyond the love commandment as law. It represents the outer circumference of the totality of our obligations to our neighbors and to God. It includes all of them but also goes beyond anything that can be specifically defined.

b) The freedom of the self over itself as contingent object in nature and history means that there is a dimension of human existence in which the preservation of the self in history becomes problematic. ("Fear not them which are able to kill the body, but rather those that are able to destroy both soul and body in hell.") The love commandment promises self-realization through self-giving ("Whosoever loseth his life will find it.") but historic success is not guaranteed in this form of self-realization. The *Agape* of Christ, which is the norm of Christian selfhood, is always finally defined as sacrificial love, as the love of the cross. ("And walk in love even as Christ loved you and gave himself for you.") Sacrificial love represents the second pinnacle of love which represents both the completion and the annulment of love as law. It is the completion of the law of love because perfect love has no logical limit short of the readiness to sacrifice the self for the other. Yet it is a point which stands beyond all law, because the necessity of sacrificing one's life for another cannot be formulated as an obligation, nor can it be achieved under the whip of the sense of obligation. Law in the determinate sense must stop with distributive justice and mutual love. Yet a sensitive conscience will have conscience pricks if another life has been taken in self-defense or if a common peril has resulted in the loss of another life but not of one's own.

Unprudential love, in which there is no calculation of mutual advantages, obviously stands in a dialectical relation to mutual love and to every scheme of distributive justice as well. In mutual love and in distributive justice the self regards itself as an equal, but not as a specially privileged, member of a group in which the rational self seeks to apportion the values of life justly or to achieve perfect reciprocity of advantages. The will to do justice is a form of love, for the interests of the neighbor are affirmed. Mutual love (*philia*) is also a form of love, for the life of the other is enhanced. Yet, on the other hand, such expressions of love fall short of love in its ultimate form. For they are mixed with a careful calculation of interest and advantages in which the self always claims an equal share. The final form of love is bereft of such calculation and meets the needs of the other without calculating comparative rights. Sacrificial love is therefore a form of love which transcends the limits of love. It is a form of love which cannot be embodied in any moral code. Nor can it be achieved by the compulsion of a sense of obligation. Yet common sense, not merely in Christian thought but also in the pagan reverence for heroic sacrifice, has, with spiritually shrewd instinct, recognized such heedless love as the final norm of love.

It cannot be separated from the realm of natural love (whether *Eros* or *philia*) by a neat line. It transcends the line of natural love. Yet without an element of heedless love, every form of mutual love would degenerate into a calculation of mutual advantages and every calculation of such advantages would finally generate resentment about an absence of perfect reciprocity. Aristotle tries to solve this problem by preferring friendship between equals. In the absence of equality there must be, he thinks, calculation of different types of advantage for the stronger and the weaker member of the friendship: honor for the one and help for the other. This is a nice illustration of the impossibility of finding a logical end for the love commandment within the limits of prudence. The final limits are beyond prudence and calculation; but these final limits are not neatly separated from the whole realm of mutual love and distributive justice. They tend to redeem this realm from degenerating into a competition of calculating egotists.

On the subjective side the line is equally lacking in neatness. For a sense of obligation may prompt men into a hazardous cause but the final act of sacrifice by which a soldier gives his life for his comrade is, as even the army rightly surmises, "beyond the call of duty." It is possible only by an accretion of strength to the will which is in the realm of grace.

In trying to do justice to this dialectical relation Catholicism has the advantage of recognizing that sacrificial love is related to natural love as the "perfect to the imperfect." It declares that this perfection is possible only by grace. But it makes grace to mean the "fitness" of man to embrace monastic poverty, in which he cannot

call anything his own. Thus, as in the case of the universal
dimension of love, the sacrificial dimension is a "counsel
of perfection," which means that it is yet another and more
rigorous statement of love as law. But the possibilities of
ecstatic, heedless, and unprudential completions of the
love commandment by "grace" in all kinds of human and
historic situations are obscured.

D'Arcy, who rightly insists on the dialectical relation
of sacrificial to mutual love in opposition to Nygren, spoils
the validity of his exposition by interpreting sacrificial
love as the flower of one element in human nature, the
element of *anima* as distinguished from *animus*. *Anima* is
the feminine principle in human nature, the tendency toward self-giving as opposed to the tendency toward self-
assertion. In such a formulation *Agape* is too simply the
completion of nature, and the contradiction between sacrifice and justice, between heedlessness and prudence, is
obscured.

But the error is hardly greater than the one which
is made by the Lutheran formulation. In Luther's doctrine of the Two Realms, justice is consigned completely
to the realm of law. There "nothing is known of Christ"
even as in the realm of the kingdom of heaven "nothing
is known of law, conscience, or sword." The law, in such
a rigorous dualism, does not even contain within it the
desire to do justice. It is no more than a coercive arrange-
ment which prevents mutual harm. Love, on the other
hand, is only *Agape* in its purest and most unadulterated
form, which means in a form in which it is known in

human experience only in rare moments of evangelical fervor or crisis heroism. This is why the Lutheran formulation of the relation of love to law is so irrelevant to the broad area of common experience in which one must balance claims and counterclaims and make discriminate judgments about competing interests.

Nygren's exposition of the contrast between *Agape* and natural love is not so much concerned with the contrast between *Agape* and the positive law as in Luther. But his idea of an absolute contradiction between *Agape* and *Eros* contains the same error. It is the error of a too rigorous separation of the realm of grace and the realm of nature. This separation must lead, as D'Arcy rightly observes, to a withering of both *Eros* and *Agape*. For *Eros* has no goal beyond itself. And *Agape* has no real relevance to the human situation.

The literature of the Social Gospel is filled with references to sacrificial love. Men are constantly challenged to follow the "way of the Cross" and to espouse the "Jesus way of life." But there is a curious mixture of bourgeois prudence with this pinnacle of grace. For it is assumed that a rigorous sacrifice will finally prove successful, so that a sufficient cumulation of sacrificial acts will obviate the necessity of sacrifice. Sacrifice really means the abandonment of short-range for long-range advantages. If the enemy is loved he will become a friend. If the conqueror is not resisted he will cease to be a conqueror. If the businessman sacrifices his profits he will gain greater advantages in the end, though not necessarily greater profits.

Up to a point all this is true, for the paradox of self-realization through self-giving has a promise for this life also. Only there is always an ultimate tragic possibility in sacrificial love which is obscured in this prudential version.

IV

c) Forgiveness has the same relation to punitive justice as sacrificial love to distributive justice. Forgiveness is both a completion and an annulment of punitive justice. It is its completion in the sense that a rigorous analysis of all factors involved in a wrong act will lead to an understanding both of the extenuating circumstances and the causal preconditions of the crime. Thus imaginative justice moves in the direction of forgiveness, or at least to remedial rather than punitive justice.

Yet forgiveness is finally in contradiction to punitive justice. It represents, in the words of Berdyaev, "the morality beyond morality." Jesus justifies the love of the enemy in terms of the imitation of a God whose mercy cuts across every conception of justice as rigorously as the impartialities of nature, in which the rain falls on the just and the unjust and the sun shines upon the evil and the good. In the parable of the Laborers in the Vineyard, the divine mercy is challenged for being unjust and defended because it exceeds justice. The whole doctrine of the Atonement in Christian thought contains the paradox of the relation of mercy to judgment. For the mercy of God is in His judgment and yet it is something which cancels

His wrath. There is no nice discrimination of merit and demerit in forgiveness, any more than there is a nice discrimination of interests in sacrificial love. Here law is transcended. Forgiveness seems to be purely in the realm of grace.

Yet even forgiveness comes partially into the category of love as law. For we are warned that if we forgive not men their trespasses neither will our heavenly Father forgive our trespasses. This would seem to mean that forgiveness is something we owe the erring brother as a right. Or rather it is something we owe God. But our forgiveness of our brethren is primarily a grateful response to God's forgiveness. ("And be ye kind one to another, tender-hearted, forgiving one another, even as God for Christ's sake hath forgiven you," Eph. 4.32.) Usually the New Testament presents forgiveness only as a possibility for those who are of contrite heart and whose uneasy conscience has been eased by divine forgiveness. Yet the fact that it is also presented as an obligation, which will incur the punishment of judgment if left undone, proves that even on this pinnacle of grace law is not completely transcended.

On this issue Luther is again clearest in illuminating the element of grace in the experience of forgiveness and least adequate in relating forgiveness to punitive justice. There are no diagonal lines in Luther's thought which relate mercy to punitive justice. There is therefore nothing to inspire the kind of development of punitive justice in the direction of imaginative justice which has in fact taken place in modern criminology and which proves that the "two realms" have more commerce with each other than Luther supposes.

Nygren's version of forgiveness as an aspect of *Agape* results in so sharp a distinction between justice and mercy that it leaves no place at all for discriminate judgments about justice. The distinction is so sharp that all moral distinctions in history seem to become invalid.

Modern liberalism, including Christian liberalism, tends to a sentimental version of forgiveness in which mercy has also completely triumphed over justice in such a way that responsibility of sin is denied. Sir Walter Moberly finds the final form of this sentimentality in modern psychiatry (in his book *Responsibility*).

The Catholic exposition of this pinnacle of grace in the law of love has special significance because it is one ultimate possibility of love which is not bound to the ascetic system. The love of the enemy is a possibility for all Christians but only through the help of supernatural grace. It belongs to the "counsels of perfection" which can be added to ordinary justice; but it has no dialectical relation to the schemes of justice, whereby the injustice in every scheme of justice would come under judgment.

d) The final pinnacle of grace in the realm of love is the relation between persons in which one individual penetrates imaginatively and sympathetically into the life of another. This pinnacle finds no special place in the Catholic counsels of perfection because it represents the ordinary possibilities of love above the level of justice as

defined in natural law. It is the very substance of the
realm of love in Buber's exposition of *I and Thou* and in
Brunner's *Divine Imperative*. It is, however, wrongly interpreted as the very substance of the realm of love. For
in that case love does not include the general spirit of justice which expresses itself in the structures, laws, social
arrangements, and economic forms by which men seek to
regulate the life of the community and to establish a maxi-
mum of harmony and justice.

The love which wills justice must not be excluded
from the realm of *Agape*. Brunner is in great error when
he interprets an act of personal kindness as more "Christian" than a statesmanlike scheme in the interest of justice.
Brunner's dictum that love "never seeks great things" is
capricious. It separates love too completely from the realm
of justice, though in a different way than the thought of
Nygren. A modern liberal form of this same error is to be
found in such reactionary movements as "Christian Economics," which insist that unemployment insurance is unnecessary because "Christians of sensitive conscience will
organize private charity for the needy." The effort to con-
fine *Agape* to the love of personal relations and to place all
the structures and artifices of justice outside that realm
makes Christian love irrelevant to the problems of man's
common life.

On the other hand, it is true that beyond and above
every human relation as ordered by a fixed structure of
justice, by custom, tradition, and legal enactment, there
remain indeterminate possibilities of love in the individual

and personal encounters of those who are in the structure. Whether men meet their fellow men with generosity
or with envy, with imagination or with ambitions of
dominion, is a question which cannot be fully solved by
the structure of justice which binds them to their fellow
men. Human actions can, to a degree, corrupt even the
highest structure and they can also partially redeem the
worst structure. The fact that slavery was essentially
wrong proves the invalidity of regarding structures of justice as irrelevant to love. Yet it did make a difference to
a slave whether he was subject to a kind or to a cruel
master. The institution was wrong because the disproportions of power in the institution of slavery were such that
they could predispose even decent men to unconscious
cruelties. But the most adequate institution is still only
a bare base upon which the higher experiences of love
must be built.

The commandment to love the neighbor as the self
must finally culminate in the individual experience in
which one self seeks to penetrate deeply into the mystery
of the other self and yet stand in reverence before a mystery which he has no right to penetrate. This kind of love
is a matter of law in the sense that the essential nature of
man, with his indeterminate freedom, requires that human
relations should finally achieve such an intimacy. But it
is also a matter of grace because no sense of obligation
can provide the imagination and forebearance by which
this is accomplished. Such intimacy is of course closely
related to sacrificial love, for the intermingling of life with

life predisposes to sacrificial abandonment of the claims
of the self for the needs of the other.

If the intimacy of personal friendship, in which life
is interwoven with life, is one of the pinnacles of *Agape*
is must follow that a sexual partnership has a natural basis
for such *Agape* far beyond other partnerships. The sexual
union as a parable, symbol, and basis for *Agape* has been
little appreciated in Christian thought, partly because of
a generally negative attitude toward sex which Christianity absorbed from Greek thought; and partly because
the particularity of the sexual union is suspect from the
standpoint of Christian universalism. Yet this aspect of
the relation of love beyond law to love as law has been
explored in Greek orthodoxy and has been most significantly illumined and also exaggerated by Vladimir Solovyov, who writes:

> Fully admitting . . . the high dignity of other kinds
> of love . . . we find nevertheless that only sexual love
> satisfies the two fundamental conditions without which
> there can be no abolition of selfhood through complete
> vital union with another. In all other kinds of love there
> is absent either the homogeneity between lover and be-
> loved, or the all inclusive difference of complementary
> qualities.[4]

It is significant that despite the ascetic traditions of
Roman Catholicism there are also recent efforts in Roman
thought to explore this relation between love and sexual
love. D'Arcy's *Mind and Heart of Love* sees the relation-

[4]*A Solovyov Anthology,* edited by S. L. Frank, p. 160.

ship not so much as the intimate and mutual self-giving
of both partners of the marriage union as in the feminine
impulse of self-giving. A more adequate exposition of the
significance of the mutual relation in marriage has recently been given in the Catholic treatise *Essay on Human
Love,* by Jean Guitton.

Naturally a particular relationship cannot exhaust the
meaning of *Agape,* particularly not the dimension which
expresses itself in its universalistic motif. But if any justice is to be done to particular and intimate relations, the
marriage union must receive a more positive appreciation
in Christian thought and life. The intimacy of the relation
has of course a basis in nature. But it can be endlessly
transfigured by grace, so that the possibilities of love as
law and love at the limits of law and love beyond the
limits in this partnership are identical with the general
logic of love as law and love as grace.

V

This analysis of love as law and love as transcending
law is incomplete without consideration of one further
problem: the relation of love to law as such. Law as such
is composed of norms of conduct prescribed by custom,
legal enactment, scriptural injunction, or rational intui-
tion, in which duties and obligations are prescribed without seeming reference to the ultimate spirit of law, namely,
love. What is the standing of such law in a Christian
scheme of ethics and how is love related to it? In Catholic
thought this law is drawn from the intuitions or logical

deductions of reason, so that even the Decalogue is regarded as normative by Aquinas only in so far as it corresponds to the natural law. In Reformation thought, systematically in Calvin and less systematically in Luther,
this law is drawn from Scripture, either from explicit law,
such as the Decalogue, or from moral admonitions in various portions of Scripture which are raised to the authority
of explicit norms for the Christian life.

All such law will be found to have two characteristics: a) It states our obligations to our neighbor is minimal
and usually in negative terms. "Thou shalt not kill." "Thou
shalt not steal." b) It states our obligations to our neighbors in terms which presuppose the fact of sin and self-
interest and the complexity of claims and counterclaims
which are arbitrated by some "rule of reason" rather than
by the ultimate scruples of the law of love.

Thus the law, however conceived, accepts and regu-
lates self-interest and prohibits only the most excessive
forms of it. It does not command that we love the neighbor but only that we do not take his life or property. It
does not command that we seek our neighbor's good but
that we respect his rights. Broadly speaking, the end of
the law is justice. But we have already seen that justice
is related to love. Thus there is a dialectical relation between love and law even as there is between love beyond
law and love as law. It might be stated as follows: The
law seeks for a tolerable harmony of life with life, sin
presupposed. It is, therefore, an approximation of the law
of love on the one hand and an instrument of love on the

other hand. Consequently the distinction between law and love is less absolute and more dialectical than conceived in either Catholic or Reformation thought.

If this conclusion be correct, it follows that law, however conceived, whether drawn from Scripture (as in Reformation thought) or from rational intuitions (as in Catholicism) or from historical tradition, is less fixed and absolute than all these theories assume. The scriptural authority, below the level of love, is less valid in the realm of law than the Reformation assumes because there is always an element of historical contingency in the allegedly absolute norms of Scriptures which makes its authority questionable in a different historical context. (St. Paul's attitude toward women in the Church is a case in point.) The authority of rational "natural" law is less valid than Catholicism supposes. The whole concept of natural law rests upon a Stoic-Aristotelian rationalism which assumes fixed historical structures and norms which do not in fact exist. Furthermore, it assumes a human participation in a universal reason in which there is no ideological taint. The moral certainties of natural law in Catholic thought are all dubious. Sometimes they rest upon deductive reason. It is assumed that it is impossible to draw logical conclusions in the field of material ethics, from the formal ethical principle that good is to be done and evil avoided. But there is no guide in the formal principle of ethics about the norms of good and evil. Sometimes they rest upon the "intuitions" of reason. While there are some seemingly universal moral judgments such as the prohibition of murder, it must be noted that they are the most universal if they are the most minimal and most negative expressions of the law of love. The more specific they become the more they are suspect as "self-evident" propositions of the natural law.

Sometimes Catholic natural theory sinks to the level of eighteenth-century rationalism, which it ostensibly abhors. It regards the propositions of natural law as propositions of analytic reason. This reason analyzes the structures of nature, including human nature, and arrives at certain conclusions about what nature "intends," as, for instance, that nature intends procreation in sexual union. In this case it forgets that human nature is characterized not only by an indeterminate freedom but by an intimate and organic relation between the impulses of nature and human freedom which permits endless elaborations of human vital capacities for which it is not easy to find a simple descriptive norm.

In short, both Catholic and Reformation theory are too certain about the fixities of the norms of law. All law, whether historical, positive, scriptural, or rational, is more tentative and less independent in its authority than orthodox Christianity, whether Catholic or Protestant, supposes, even as it is more necessary than liberal Protestantism assumes. The final dyke against relativism is to be found, not in these alleged fixities, but in the law of love itself. This is the only final law, and every other law is an expression of the law of love in minimal or in proximate terms or in terms appropriate to given historical occasions.

11. *Coherence, Incoherence, and Christian Faith*

THE WHOLE OF reality is characterized by a basic coherence. Things and events are in a vast web of relationships and are known through their relations. Perceptual knowledge is possible only within a framework of conceptual images, which in some sense conform to the structures in which reality is organized. The world is organized or it could not exist; if it is to be known, it must be known through its sequences, coherences, casualties, and essences.

The impulse to understand the world expresses itself naturally in the movement toward metaphysics, rising above physics; in the desire to penetrate behind and above the forms and structures of particular things to the form and structure of being per se. It is natural to test the conformity to the particular coherence in which it seems to

belong. We are skeptical about ghosts, for instance, because they do not conform to the characteristics of historical reality as we know it.

We instinctively assume that there is only one world
and that it is a cosmos, however veiled and unknown its
ultimate coherences, incongruities, and contradictions in
life, in history, and even in nature. In the one world there
are many worlds, realms of meaning and coherence; and
these are not easily brought into a single system. The
worlds of mind and matter have been a perennial problem
in ontology, as have subject and object in epistemology.
There must be a final congruity between these realms,
but most of the rational theories of their congruity tend
to obscure some truth about each realm in the impulse to
establish total coherence. The effort to establish simple
coherence may misinterpret specific realities in order to
fit them into a system. There are four primary perils to
truth in making coherence the basic test of truth.

1.   Things and events may be too unique to fit into
any system of meaning; and their uniqueness is destroyed
by a premature coordination to a system of meaning, particularly a system which identifies meaning with rationality. Thus there are historical characters and events, con-
cretions and configurations, which the romantic tradition
tries to appreciate in their uniqueness in opposition to
simpler and neater systems of meaning which obscure the
uniqueness of the particular. There are also unique moral
situations which do not fit simply into some general rule
of natural law.

2. Realms of coherence and meaning may stand in rational contradiction to each other; and they are not fully understood if the rational contradiction is prematurely resolved as, for instance, being and becoming, eternity and time. Thus the classical metaphysics of being could not appreciate the realities of growth and becoming, the emergence of novelty, in short historical development; and modern metaphysics has equal difficulty in finding a structure of the permanent and the perennial in the flux of becoming (Bergson versus Aristotle). The problem of time and eternity is not easily solved in rational terms. Hegel invented a new logic to comprehend becoming as integral to being; but his system could not do justice to the endless possibilities of novelty and surprise in historical development. He prematurely rationalized time and failed to do justice to genuine novelty.

3. There are configurations and structures which stand athwart every rationally conceived system of meaning and cannot be appreciated in terms of the alternative efforts to bring the structure completely into one system or the other. The primary example is man himself, who is both in nature and above nature and who has been alternately misunderstood by naturalistic and idealistic philosophies. Idealism understands his freedom as mind but not his reality as contingent object in nature. It elaborates a history of man as if it were a history of mind, without dealing adequately with man as determined by geography and climate, by interest and passion. Naturalism, on the other hand, tells the history of human culture as if it were

a mere variant of natural history. These same philosophies are of course equally unable to solve the problem presented by the incongruity of mind and matter in ontology and of subject and object in epistemology. The one tries to reduce mind to matter or to establish a system of psychophysical parallelism. The other seeks to derive the world of objects from the world of mind. The inconclusive debate between them proves the impossibility of moving rationally from mind to matter or matter to mind in ontology or of resolving the epistemological problem rationally. There is no rational refutation of subjective idealism. It is resolved by what Santayana calls "animal faith." All science rests upon the common-sense faith that the processes of mind and the processes of nature are relevant to each other.

4. Genuine freedom, with the implied possibility of violating the natural and rational structures of the world, cannot be conceived in any natural or rational scheme of coherence. This furnishes a second reason for the misunderstanding of man and his history in all rational schemes. The whole realm of genuine selfhood, of sin and of grace, is beyond the comprehension of various systems of philosophy. Neither Aristotle nor Kant succeeds in accounting for the concrete human self as free agent. This mystery of human freedom, including the concomitant mystery of historic evil, plus the previous incongruity of man both as free spirit and as a creature of nature, led Pascal to elaborate his Christian existentialism in opposition to the Cartesian rationalism and Jesuit Thomism of

his day. Pascal delved "in mysteries without which man remains a mystery to himself"; and that phrase may be a good introduction to the consideration of the relation of the suprarational affirmations of the Christian faith to the antinomies, contradictions, and mysteries of human existence.

II

The question to be considered is in what way these suprarational affirmations are related to and validated by their capacity to resolve and clarify the antinomies, the aspects of uniqueness and particularity, the obscure meanings and tangents of meaning in human life and history.

Judged by any standard of coherence and compared with other high religions, Christianity seems to be a primitive religion because all of these are more, rather than less, rigorous than science and philosophy in their effort to present the world and life as a unified whole and to regard all discords and incongruities as provisional or illusory. Of the high religions, only Christianity and Judaism and possibly Zoroastrianism may be defined as historical religions. Perhaps Mohammedanism could be included as a legalistic version of historical religion. All other religions, including the mystic version of Mohammedanism—Sufism—could be defined as culture religions in which a universal principle of meaning is sought either within the structures of the world or within some universal subsistence above and beyond the structures. These culture religions are, to use Oman's distinction, pantheistic in either the cosmic or the acosmic sense.

Cosmic forms of pantheism are religious versions of various metaphysical systems, idealistic and naturalistic, in which the ultimate religious issue implied in the ontological quest is made explicit. Stoicism is a naturalistic form of pantheism in so far as it presents the world as a vast rational order to which human life must conform. In so far as Stoicism has a "reason within us" to which we may flee from the reason within the world, it tends to an acosmic form of pantheism. Spinozism is a more consistently naturalistic version of pantheism. Modern naturalism is a form of pantheism in which the temporal process needs no longer to be explained but becomes the principle of the explanation of all things. In the thought of Bergson the religious veneration for time as a source of meaning is explicit. He believes it possible to penetrate to it as a source of the meaning of life by a kind of mystic identification, to be distinguished from conceptual knowledge.

Acosmic forms of pantheism, whether Neo-Platonism, Brahmanism, or Buddhism, are distinguished from cosmic forms by placing the mystery of consciousness outside the rational or natural coherence of the world. Sensing a deeper mystery of spirit than will fit into either the concepts of nature or of mind, they practice a technique of introversion by which the self as subject extricates itself endlessly from the self as contingent object (the mind as well as the physical self being reduced to the level of the

temporal world) until the self has achieved the universality
of the divine. The divine is significantly an undifferentiated ground and goal, which underlies all things. In such
mysticism the drive toward coherence has taken its most
consistent form. From the standpoint of this pure mysticism the whole temporal world, with all its particular
events and objects, including the particular self, is reduced to essential meaninglessness. Buddhism may be regarded as the most consistent form of this drive toward
the ultimate in culture religion, which ends with a vision
of a Nirvana which is at once the fulness of existence and
nonexistence. This is the kind of spirituality in which Al-
dous Huxley seeks a refuge from the twentieth century.
In contrast to this logic of culture religions the emphases
in the Christian faith upon the unique, the contradictory,
the paradoxical, and the unresolved mystery is striking.
The temporal world comes into existence through God's
creation. The concept of creation defines the mystery beyond both natural and rational causalities, and its suprarational character is underscored when Christian theology
is pressed to accept the doctrine of creation *ex nihilo*.
Thereby a realm of freedom and mystery is indicated beyond the capacity of reason to comprehend. This is where
reason starts and ends. The final irrationality of the give-
ness of things is frankly accepted.

On the other end of time is the culmination of the
world in a transfigured time. As von Hügel rightly asserts,
biblical eschatology must adhere to the rational absurdity
that there will be time in eternity, that our partial simul-

taneity will not be annulled by God's *totum simul,* that
the culmination means not the annulment but the fulfilment of the temporal process. In Cullmann's *Christ and
Time* the biblical concept of a new aeon, a new time, is
interpreted even more radically but probably too radically.
These conceptions of alpha and omega, of beginning and
end, are rationally absurd, or at least paradoxical, but they
guard the Christian interpretation of life from both an
empty heaven and an impossible utopia, from either a
meaningless time or a self-fulfilling time. They are, however, only the frame for the more positive content of the
Christian message. Every tendency to make the Christian
revelation mean primarily the invasion of time by the
eternal (as in some doctrines of the Incarnation) obscures
this more positive content of the Christian Gospel which
has to do with man's and God's freedom, with man's sin
and God's grace.

The Christian answer to the human predicament, a
divine mercy toward man, revealed in Christ, which is
at once a power enabling the self to realize itself truly
beyond itself in love, and the forgiveness of God toward
the self which even at its best remains in partial contradiction to the divine will, is an answer which grows out
of, and which in turn helps to create, the radical Christian
concept of human freedom. In the Christian faith the self
in its final freedom does not find its norm in the structures
either of nature or of reason. Nor is either able to bind
the self's freedom or guarantee its virtue, as the proponents of "natural law" would have it. The principle of

rationality, the force of logic, does not secure the virtue of the self, as in the thought of Kant. For the self can make use of logic for its ends. The partial and particular self is not merely a provisional particularity which is overcome in the universal self which develops with increasing rationality. Nor is the evil in the self the provisional confusion and cross-purposes of natural passion before ordered by mind as in Aristotle. There is, in other words, no form, structure, or logos, in nature to which the self ought to return from its freedom and no such form within its reason which would guarantee that the self will express itself harmoniously with the total structure of existence above the level of natural necessity. The self is free to defy God. The self does defy God. The Christian conception of the dignity of man and of the misery of man is all of one piece, as Pascal rightly apprehended. All Renaissance and modern emphases upon the dignity of man to the exclusion of the Christian conception of the sin of man are lame efforts to reconstruct the Christian doctrine of selfhood without understanding the full implications of the Christian conception of the self's freedom.

But the Christian doctrine of selfhood means that neither the life of the individual self nor the total drama of man's existence upon earth can be conceived in strictly rational terms of coherence. Each is a drama of an engagement between the self and God and between mankind and God, in which all sorts of events may happen. The only certainty from a Christian standpoint is that evil cannot rise to the point of defeating God; that every form of egotism, self-idolatry, and defiance stands under divine judgment; that this judgment is partially executed in actual history, though not in complete conformity with the divine righteousness, so that history remains morally ambiguous to the end; and that a divine redemptive love is always initiating a reconciliation between God and man. According to this answer, a suffering divine love is the final coherence of life. This love bears within itself the contradictions and cross-purposes made possible by human freedom. To a certain degree this answer reaches down to cover even the antinomies known as natural evil. There is no possibility of defining the created world as good if the test of goodness is perfect harmony. A too-strict identification of goodness with coherence must always lead to a conception of nature which is on the brink of interpreting nature and the temporal as evil because there is conflict in it.

It must be noted that the Christian answer, adequate for a full understanding of both the good and the evil possibilities of human freedom, involves a definition of God which stands beyond the limits of rationality. God is defined as both just and merciful, with His mercy at once the contradiction to and the fulfilment of His justice. He is defined in trinitarian terms. The Almighty creator, who transcends history, and the redeemer who suffers in history are two and yet one. The Holy Spirit, who is the final bond of unity in the community of the redeemed, represents not the rational harmony of all things in their nature but the ultimate harmony, which includes both the power of the creator and the love of the redeemer. Christian theology has sought through all the ages to make both the Doctrine of the Atonement and the Trinity rationally explicable. This enterprise can never be completely successful, except in the sense that Alternative propositions can be proved to be too simple solutions. Without the atonement all religious conceptions of justice degenerate into legalism and all conceptions of love into sentimentality. Without the Trinity, the demands of a rigorous logic do not stop short of pantheism.

In short, the situation is that the ultrarational pinnacles of Christian truth, embodying paradox and contradiction and straining at the limits of rationality, are made plausible when understood as the keys which make the drama of human life and history comprehensible and without which it is either given a too-simple meaning or falls into meaninglessness. Thus existentialism is a natural revolt against the too-simple meanings of traditional rationalism, and logical positivism expresses a skepticism too radically obscured by idealism.

III

A Christian apologetic which validates the suprarational affirmations of meaning by proving them to be the source of meaning for the seeming contradictions and antinomies of life runs through the whole of Scripture. The Book of Deuteronomy is full of warnings against a too rational conception of the covenant; for that would lead to the conviction that Israel has been chosen either because of its power or because of its virtue. No reason but God's mysterious grace can be given for the covenant. In the Book of Job the attempt to measure God's goodness by human standards of justice is rebuked. The Second Isaiah never tires of reminding Israel of the inscrutable and yet meaningful character of the divine sovereignty over history. Every simple moral conception of it would make the tortuous course of history seem completely meaningless, since it does not conform to a simple moral pattern. It is in searching for the ultimate meaning of the morally intolerable suffering of righteous and comparatively innocent Israel that Chapter 53 of Isaiah first establishes the relation between a moral obscurity in history with what becomes in the New Testament the final clarification of the moral obscurity of history, a suffering God. Paul rejoices in the fact that what seems foolishness from the standpoint of the world's wisdom, the message of the Cross, becomes in the eyes of faith the key which unlocks the mysteries of life and makes sense out of it. It is, furthermore, power as well as wisdom, because the faith to apprehend this true wisdom requires repentance, which is to say a destruction of all false systems of meaning in which the self has exalted itself against the knowledge of God, by idolatrous confidence in its own wisdom or its own power.

The perennial question in Christian apologetics is how these validations of the truths of the Christian faith are to be related to the wisdom of the world, to the cultural disciplines which seek on various levels to find the congruities and coherences the structures and forms of nature, life, and history.

On the one hand, there is a tradition of Christian theology which glories in the contradiction between the foolishness of God and the wisdom of men. It runs from Tertullian, through Augustine, Occam, Duns Scotus, to the Reformation, Pascal, Kierkegaard, and Barth.

Luther speaks for this tradition in the words: "We know that reason is the devil's harlot and can do nothing but slander all that God says and does. If outside of Christ you wish by your own thoughts to know your relation to God you will break your neck.—Therefore keep to revelation and do not try to understand."

The other tradition runs from Origen through Aquinas, the Christian Platonists, the Renaissance Humanists, to modern liberal Christianity. For this tradition Aquinas speaks: "The natural dictates of reason must certainly be true. It is impossible to think of their being otherwise, nor again is it possible to believe that the tenets of faith are false. Since falsehood alone is contrary to truth it is impossible for the truths of faith to be contrary to the principles known by reason."

The inconclusive character of the debate between these two schools may be due to the tendency of one side to make the suprarational affirmations of faith too simply irrational. Being unconcerned with the disciplines of culture and the validity of their search for provisional coherences, they miss the opportunity to find the point where such coherences reveal their own limits and turn sense into nonsense by seeking to comprehend the incongruous too simply in a system of rational coherence.

The Christian rationalists, on the other hand, equate meaning too simply with rationality and thereby inevitably obscure some of the profoundest incongruities, tragic antinomies, and depth of meaning on the edge of the mysteries in human life and history. There is a certain logic in the rise and fall of theological systems. Thomism achieves its triumph in the stabilities of the thirteenth century, while the Renaissance spirituality culminating in liberal Protestantism is victorious in the nineteenth-century heyday of the middle-class world in which this type of spirituality arose. Each becomes irrelevant in the historic disintegrations of the fourteenth and twentieth centuries in which things hidden become revealed. This is not to suggest that the basic problems of human existence are essentially different in ages of tranquility than in ages of tragedy. It is merely to suggest that there are aspects of human existence which are more clearly seen and recognized when the relatively rational harmonies of social existence of a stable period prove themselves less typical of the whole human situation than they appeared to be.

In Thomism the suprarational truths of faith are not identified with the truths of reason. They illumine a realm of mystery above and beyond the limits of the world which is rationally understood and morally ordered. The existence of God is known by reason, but His character as triune God is apprehended by faith. This means that the finiteness of man's reason and its involvement in the flux of the temporal world is not appreciated. In the realm of morality the rational man feels secure in the virtue which he may achieve by his reason and the justice which he can define by it. This means that the problematic character of all human virtues and the ideological taint in all reasoning about human affairs are not understood. Therefore, grace becomes merely an addition to natural virtue and in no way stands in contradiction to it. Significantly man is essentially defined as a rational creature, just as Aristotle would define him. The true dimension of selfhood, with its indeterminate relations to itself, to God, and to its fellow-men, is regarded as an addition, a *donum superadditum.* Wherever one touches the Thomistic scheme, one finds a perfectly coherent world, a perfectly understood self, a perfectly possible virtue and justice. This coherent world has superimposed upon it an aura of mystery and meaning in which the limitless possibilities of man's and God's freedom find expression. It is a two-story world with a classical base and a Christian second story.

The general picture of faith's relation to culture, of the Gospel's relation to the wisdom of the world, in the world view of the Renaissance and subsequently in liberal Protestantism represents one further step toward the acceptance of a rationally coherent world. The mystery of creation is resolved in the evolutionary concept. "Some call it evolution and others call it God." The Bible becomes a library, recording in many books the evolutionary ascent of man to God. Sin becomes the provisional inertia of impulses inherited from Neanderthal man against the wider purposes of mind. Christ is the symbol of history itself, as in Hegel. The relation of the Kingdom of God to the moral perplexities and ambiguities of history is resolved in utopia. The strict distinction between justice and love in Catholic thought is marvelously precise and shrewd, compared with the general identification of the agape of the New Testament with the "community-building capacities of human sympathy" (Rauschenbusch). This reduction of the ethical meaning of the scandal of the Cross, namely, sacrificial love, to the dimensions of simple mutuality imparts an air of sentimentality to all liberal Protestant social and political theories. Usually nothing is added to the insights of the sociology of Comte or Spencer. At only one point is modern humanism transcended. The self must pray to express itself fully, but this prayer usually assumes a simple harmony between our highest aspirations and God's will. If Catholic thought represents a layer cake with a base of classical rationalism, this Christian liberalism in its most consistent form is a confection in which the whole cake comes from the modern temporal world view. The icing is Christian; and the debate between the secular or the Christian version is usually on the question whether the icing is too sweet or whether the cake would be more wholesome with or without the icing. All the tragic antinomies of history, the inner contradictions of human existence, and the ultimate mysteries of time and eternity are obscured. It is not easy to determine whether the antinomies and contradictions of human life and history have been obscured because the Christian frame of reference through which they could be seen has been disavowed or whether this faith has been disavowed because it answered questions and resolved contradictions which were no longer felt.

Matthew Arnold illustrates the emphasis on congruity in the confluence of Christian and secular types of modern spirituality. He thought that the coincidence of virtue and happiness was the final proof of the truth of Christianity. The idealist Bradley made sport of this conviction, pointing out that nothing was more dubious than the idea of such a coincidence. He should have noted, however, that the idea of such a coincidence is as foreign to the Christian faith as it is untrue to experience. "This is thankworthy, if a man for conscience toward God endure grief, suffering wrongfully. For what glory is it, if, when ye be buffeted for your faults, ye shall take it patiently? But if ye do well and suffer for it, ye take it patiently, this is acceptable with God" (I Pet. 2:19).

IV

It is obviously perilous both to the content of the Christian faith and to the interpretation of life to place such reliance on the coherences and rationalities, the sequences and harmonies, of nature and reason. But the perils in the other direction are vividly displayed in contemporary as well as older Christian existentialism. The primary peril is that the wisdom of the Gospel is emptied of meaning by setting it into contradiction to the wisdom of the world and denying that the coherences and realms of meaning which the cultural disciplines rightfully analyze and establish have any relation to the Gospel.

Kierkegaard's protest against Hegelianism betrays him into a position in which all inquiries into essences, universal forms, are discounted in order to emphasize the existing particular. The existing individual is the only particular in history with its own internal history. Others, have no internal history and therefore no integral individuality, which could be known existentially. They must be known by fitting them into genus and species.

Kierkegaard, furthermore, exploits the inner contradiction within man as free spirit and contingent object too simply as the basis of faith. According to him, the individual, by embracing this contradiction in passionate subjectivity, rather than by evading it, comes truly to himself, chooses himself in his absolute validity. Though the writings of Kierkegaard contain a genuine expression of the Christian faith and are an exposition of the Pauline statement, "That I might know him, no rather that I might be known of him," there are notes in Kierkegaard's thought according to which the self really saves itself by choosing itself in its absolute validity. Sometimes this means that passionate subjectivity becomes the sole test of truth in such a way that a disinterested worship of an idol is preferred to the wrong worship of the true God. This allows for a justified condemnation of a false worship of God, but it also lacks any standard by which the true God could be distinguished from a false one. In other words, a passionate Nazi could meet Kierkegaard's test. There are standards of judgment in Renaissance and liberal universalism which make their ethic preferable to this kind of hazardous subjectivity.

Sometimes Kierkegaard does choose a rigorous universalism to express the ethical life of the self in its absolute validity. In his *Works of Love* Christian love is universal love, expressed as a sense of duty. It is a universalism almost identical with Kant's dictum that we must make our actions the basis of universal law. But there is no grace, no freedom, no release in it. It is full of the sweat of a plodding righteousness, and it hides the fact of the self's continued finiteness.

Both errors, though seemingly contradictory, prove that the problems of life have been solved too simply by embracing the inner contradiction in human existence and not by a genuine commerce of repentance and faith between finite and sinful man and the grace of God. It is a warning that we cannot simply equate the Christian faith with a philosophy which embodies particularity and contradiction rather than one which obscures the particular and the contradictory.

These perils in Kierkegaard's existentialism may have helped to drive Barth more and more in another direction. He will explore neither the inner contradictions of life nor the coherences and congruities of which philosophy speaks, for apologetic purposes. Ethically Barth is as relativist as Westermarck and epistemologically as much a positivist as Carnap. Man does not know anything of significance. The Word of God is the only light which shines into his darkness, and its acceptance or nonacceptance is a pure mystery of grace. The sower merely sows upon all sorts of fields without inquiring whether it is this or that kind of ground, or whether a word of hope must be spoken to life in despair or a word of judgment to life caught in conventional complacency.

This means that the whole commerce between the foolishness of the Gospel and the wisdom of the world, between faith and culture, is disavowed. The truth of the Gospel does not stand at the limits of human wisdom. For there is no real content in this wisdom. One could not, for instance, from this standpoint engage in a debate with psychologists on the question of what level of human selfhood is adequately illumined by psychiatric techniques and what level of the self as subject and free spirit evades these analyses. Nor could one debate with social scientists on the possibilities and the limits of a rational justice in human society.

The exposition of the Christian faith, lacking this commerce with culture, becomes more and more literalistic and allegorical, since its only purpose can be to explain the inner coherence of the Scripture. In this enterprise the fruits of historical scholarship are dealt with in more and more cavalier fashion, and the Old Testament is finally emptied of its most significant meanings, for these are related to particular points in history. An allegorical relation to Christ must be found in order to establish an immediate contact between the center of the spiritual truth and every word of Scripture. This is no longer *Heilsgeschichte* but one vast allegory. The ethical consequences of this lack of dialogue between the disciplines of culture and the Christian faith are equally revealing. Barth declares it to be one of the mysteries of divine providence that a civil society should, despite the ideological taint on all its concepts of justice, yet achieve a measure of justice. This means that, with Thomas Hobbes, he arrives at the false conclusion that natural man has no capacity to consider interests other than his own. In short, he applies a doctrine of total depravity to the political realm, and therefore he cannot deal with the actualities of politics, which represent bewildering mixtures of idealism and self-interest, of the sense of justice and the inclination to injustice. We cannot afford to obscure the rational coherences in man's social life, however imperfect.

In this world Barth bids the Christian Church to witness to the resurrection; that is, to set up signs and symbols of redemption in the confusion of sin. His signs are all explicitly eschatological. They must have something of the aura of martyrdom upon them. He bids the Church to wait until the issues are clear before it bears this heroic witness, just as he himself waited in witnessing against Hitlerism until the manifest injustices of a tyrannical state revealed their clearly idolatrous religious character. This is a religion, as a Catholic critic rightly observes, which is fashioned for the catacombs and has little relation to the task of transfiguring the natural stuff of politics by the grace and wisdom of the Gospel.

In the realm of apologetics Barth never explores the character of the wisdom of the world in its ambivalence between the idolatrous glorification of some particular center of meaning and the mystical search for an end which is free of idolatry but also empty of meaning. It is in this ambivalence that the true pathos of culture religion is to be found. For Barth all natural religion represents idolatry, the false worship of the collective self as God. Actually there is, as Paul observed, a yearning for the true, the more ultimate, the unknown God beyond and above all the known gods of idolatry. It was at this point that Paul found a point of contact between the Gospel and the religious yearnings of mankind. These religious yearnings do not yield a Gospel. But they delineate the dimension of the human situation which makes the message of the Gospel relevant.

There is, in short, no possibility of fully validating the truth in the foolishness of the Gospel if every cultural discipline is not taken seriously up to the point where it becomes conscious of its own limits and the point where the insights of various disciplines stand in contradiction to each other, signifying that the total of reality is more complex than any scheme of rational meaning which may be invented to comprehend it.

These criticisms of the two best-known forms of Christian existentialism imply a third position which would distinguish itself from both by taking the coherences and causalities of life and history more seriously than Kierkegaard. On the other hand, it rejects the biblical literalism into which Barth is betrayed and his attitude toward the disciplines of philosophy and the sciences. We might well define this position as biblical realism. The general outlines of such a position are at least negatively defined in the criticisms which have been made here of both the two forms of Christian rationalism and the two forms of Christian existentialism. One dilemma of such a position must be mentioned in conclusion. It is the one which gives a certain validity to the term "neo-orthodoxy."

If we take the disciplines of the various sciences seriously, as we do, we must depart at one important point from the biblical picture of life and history. The accumulated evidence of the natural sciences convinces us that the realm of natural causation is more closed, and less subject to divine intervention, than the biblical world view assumes. We can be completely biblical in interpreting the drama of human history as an engagement between man and God. We can see it, as neither the rationalists nor the naturalists can, as open to indeterminate possibilities of good and of evil. We can recognize in the course of history particular events which have a special depth and penetrate to the meaning of the whole, that is, revelation.

But meanwhile this history has a base in nature as man himself has. And the course of nature is more subject to inflexible law than the Bible supposes. In other words, we have given up one kind of miracle, and miracle is the dearest child of faith. We do not have difficulty with all miracles. The healing miracles of Jesus, for instance, are credible because we recognize the depth and height of spirit in the dimension of each personality and the consequent spiritual dimension of bodily ill. Psychosomatic medicine corroborates such a conception. But we do not believe in the virgin birth, and we have difficulty with the physical resurrection of Christ. We do not believe, in other words, that revelatory events validate themselves by a divine break-through in the natural order. There is a great spiritual gain in this position which is in accord with Christ's own rejection of signs and wonders as validations of his messianic mission. ("This wicked generation seeketh a sign.") It leads to an apprehension of the points of revelation by repentance and faith, that is to say, it insists that the truth of revelation must be apprehended by the whole person and cannot merely be accepted as a historical fact, validated by the miraculous character of the fact. The deeper truth must be apprehended by becoming the key which unlocks the mystery of what man is and should be and of what God is in relations with men.

Yet there is a peril in this way of interpreting the Gospel truth. The peril lies in the tendency to reduce Christianity to yet another philosophy, profounder than other philosophies because it embodies heights and depths which are not comprehended in the others. We say we take historical facts seriously but not literally; but that may be on the way of not taking them as historical facts at all. Thus we reject the myth of the fall of man as a historical fact. With that rejection we can dispose of all nonsense about a biologically inherited corruption of sin. But we also easily interpret human evil as an inevitable condition of human finiteness and stand on the edge of Platonism, or, by rejecting the end of the world as a literal event, we easily obscure the eternity at the end of time and have only an eternity over time left, again a movement toward Platonism.

There is no simple solution for this problem. It is to be noted that the great Christian existentialists, Pascal, Luther, Kierkegaard, thought in a world in which modern science had not radically altered or was just beginning to alter the conception of nature. Modern Barthians blithely disregard the evidences of modern science as if they did not exist.

If a solution is to be found in modern apologetics it must rest upon two primary propositions. 1) A radical distinction between the natural world and the world of human history must be made, however much history may have a natural base. The justification for this distinction lies in the unique character of human freedom. Almost all the misinterpretations of human selfhood and the drama of history in the modern day are derived from the effort to reduce human existence to the coherence of nature. 2) Human history must be understood as containing within it the encounters between man and God in which God intervenes to reconstruct the rational concepts of meaning which men and cultures construct under the false assumption that they have a mind which completely transcends the flux of history, when actually it can only construct a realm of meaning from a particular standpoint within the flux. The true God is encountered in a) creativities which introduce elements into the historic situation which could not have been anticipated. "God takes the things that are not to put to naught the things that are." In history this creativity appears as grace, as a form of election for which no reason can be given, as in God's covenant with Israel. If a reason is given for such events, they are falsely brought into a premature realm of coherence. b) God is encountered in judgment whenever human ideals, values, and historical achievements are discovered to be in contradiction to the divine rather than in simple harmony with the ultimate coherence of things. Included in such historical events are the prophetic testimonies which fathom the contradiction between the human and divine. God speaks to the believer not only in mighty acts but through the testimony of the prophets ("God who spoke aforetime through the prophets"). The prophet Jeremiah significantly makes the promise of security for a particular historic stability ("Ye shall have assured peace in this place") into a test of false prophecy. No reason for these prophetic insights can be given. They are not anticipated by the highest culture, but they can by faith be incorporated into a new interpretation of the meaning of history. c) Events in which the divine judgments lead to a reconstitution of life. These are revelations of redeeming grace in which the old self, including the collective self of false cultures, is destroyed, but the destruction leads to newness of life. The Bible rightly represents the whole drama of Christ as the final point in *Heilsgeschichte,* for here every form of human goodness is revealed in its problematic character. But a recognition of that fact makes a new form of goodness possible. If we are baptized into Christ's death, we may rise with him to newness of life.

These historic events come to the believer as given. They can therefore not be anticipated by any philosophy of coherence. They presuppose an existential incoherence between human striving and the divine will. They can be appropriated only by faith, that is, existentially rather than speculatively, because the recognition of their truth requires a repentant attitude toward false completions of life from the human standpoint. Furthermore, they assert a relevance between a divine freedom and a human freedom, across the chasm of the inflexibilities of nature which have no other message but death, to this curious animal, man, who is more than an animal. These historic revelations can be related speculatively to the various aspects of human existence and can make sense out of them. Reason can thus follow after faith. It can also precede it, in the sense that a highly sophisticated reason can point to the limits of rational coherence in understanding contradictory aspects of reality and more particularly to the dimension of the human spirit which cannot be understood without presupposing a dimension of divine freedom above the coherences of nature and mind as its environment; which in its endless self-transcendence knows that all judgments passed upon it by history are subject to a more ultimate judgment ("He that judges me is the Lord"); and, finally, which is abortively involved in overcoming the incongruity of its existence as free spirit and as object in nature, either by denying its freedom (sensuality) or by denying its finiteness (hybris). For this sin, when acknowledged, there is a cure, a humble and a charitable life. That testimony can enter into history as a proof of the Christian faith, which the unbelievers may see. But if it should be true that even the most righteous life remains in some degree of contradiction to the divine, it is hazardous either for individual Christians or the Church to point to their goodness as proofs of the truth of their faith. The final answer to this incoherence between the human and the divine will is the divine suffering mercy; and for this no reason can be given.

It is significant that the negative proofs of the Christian faith are not lost on the most sophisticated moderns who have recognized the inadequacy of the smooth pictures of man and history in modern culture. "It cannot be denied," writes an historian, "that Christian analyses of human conduct and of human history are truer to the facts of experience than alternative analyses." But, he adds, "whether the truth of these analyses can be derived only from presuppositions of the Christian faith remains to be determined."

Thus on the positive side we are where we have always been. Faith is not reason. It is the substance of things hoped for, the evidence of things not seen. The situation for faith is only slightly altered by the new picture of a quasi-autonomous nature, created by God, not maintained by His fiat from moment to moment. No sign can be given but that of the prophet Jonah, by which Jesus meant the sign of death and resurrection. This is to say, whenever the vicissitudes from which the self, either individually or collectively, suffers are appropriated by faith as divine judgments and not as meaningless caprice, they result in the love, joy, and peace of a new life.

This faith in the sovereignty of a divine creator, judge, and redeemer is not subject to rational proof, because it stands beyond and above the rational coherences of the world and can therefore not be proved by an analysis of these coherences. But a scientific and philosophical analysis of these coherences is not incapable of revealing where they point beyond themselves to a freedom which is not in them, to contradictions between each other which suggest a profounder mystery and meaning beyond them. A theology which both holds fast to the mystery and meaning beyond these coherences and also has a decent respect for the order and meaning of the natural world cannot be a queen of the sciences, nor should she be the despised and neglected handmaiden of her present estate. Her proper position is that of the crucified Lord, who promises to come again with great power and glory. The power and glory are not a present possession. That is indicated by the fact that the accusers and crucifiers must always pay inadvertent tribute to the kingdom of truth, which they seek to despise.